EASY SPEEDY VEGAN

KATY BESKOW

EASY
SPEEDY
VEGAN

100 Quick Plant-Based Recipes

KATY BESKOW

Photography by Luke Albert

Hardie Grant

QUADRILLE

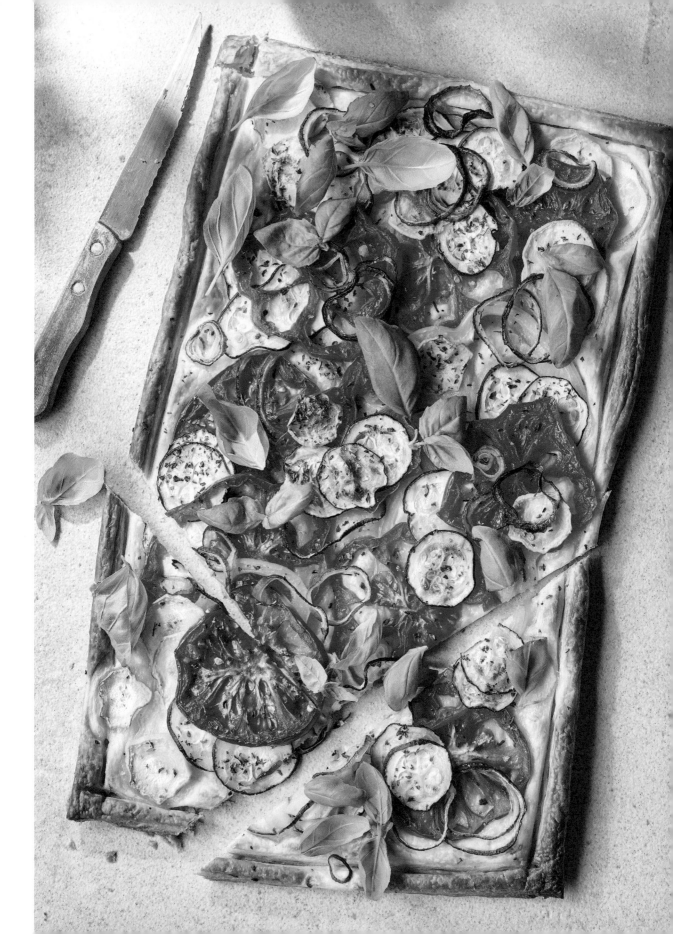

CONTENTS

Introduction 8
Kitchen hacks 11
The speedy store cupboard
   and fuss-free fridge 12

10 MINUTES 20

20 MINUTES 82

30 MINUTES 144

Time index 212
General index 214
Acknowledgements 222

INTRODUCTION

What do you do when you've got less than half an hour to cook a meal? Reach for the takeaway menu? Search the freezer for that supermarket ready meal? Give up and make a crisp sandwich? We've all been there (myself included), along with the longing for a freshly cooked meal that soon follows.

Since I became a vegan back in 2006, I've been cooking up quick and simple meals that had to fit my busy lifestyle. With no time (or desire) to simmer beans and pulses for hours, I used shortcuts and techniques to create homely, delicious and balanced dishes. I love sharing these recipes with you through my website and collection of books, and this time I wanted to create something more personalized to your time as well as taste, with *Easy Speedy Vegan*.

The increase in availability of vegan convenience foods is to be celebrated, making veganism visible and accessible to many more people. But convenience comes at a cost: financially within your weekly shopping bills, to the planet with excess packaging, and also to your creativity in the kitchen if you rely solely on prepared meals. Realistically, it's unlikely that we can all cook from scratch seven days a week, for three meals a day – life gets in the way, no matter how hard we try. So, in this collection of 100 recipes, I've included something for every time of day, every mood, and to suit your own time frame.

To get the most out of this book, simply consider how much time you have available to cook, whether it's 10, 20 or 30 minutes. Select the chapter that best suits the time you have, then choose the recipe that takes your fancy. Each chapter has recipes suitable for breakfast, lunch, supper and dessert, so there's something to inspire you at any time of the day, no matter how little time you have. I've also labelled which recipes are suitable for freezing, so you can save any leftovers for another day, or batch cook for your future self.

This book is created around you, and the time you want to spend cooking, whether it's just for yourself, or a supper for family and friends. Instead of wasting time searching for recipes that are quick to cook, allow this more personalized approach to meet your needs and the actual time you have available. I hope you enjoy cooking and eating these meals as much as I enjoyed creating them!

KITCHEN HACKS

I know that you're busy and short of time, so here are my favourite kitchen hacks for speedy cooking and a fuss-free experience in the kitchen.

- **If a recipe calls for the oven to be used**, the first thing you should do is switch it on and get it up to temperature while you prepare the ingredients. An oven preheated to the correct temperature (this will take 5–15 minutes depending on your oven) will be ready to cook your food from the moment it goes in, without risking uneven heating or longer cooking times.

- **Use good-quality knives** that sit ergonomically in your hand, for easy chopping, slicing and dicing. You don't need a large selection of knives: one small, medium and large, and also a bread knife, will serve your needs. Use a wooden chopping board to protect your knives, and to make ingredient preparation easy and clean. A food processor (if you have one) does all the hard slicing, dicing and grating for you, but do factor in the cleaning time of this appliance when you're short on time.

- **High-powered jug blenders** whip up the silkiest soups and sauces in next to no time, with minimal effort from you. A simple hand-held stick blender is a space saver, but will require a little more time and effort to achieve a smooth result.

- **Have a selection of freezer-safe containers** to hand, to store and freeze any leftovers. Not only are you reducing food waste and saving money, but you're preparing a meal for another day. When you have time available, batch cook a few meals and freeze them, ready for when you know you won't even have the time (or energy) to whip up even a 10-minute meal. Homemade meals will last for about 3 months in the freezer, and be sure to label the container with the name of the dish and the date it was cooked (it can be difficult to distinguish once frozen).

- **Keep a few store cupboard essentials available** (page 12) so you can create easy meals in next to no time. It's handy to have a selection of simple spice pastes, chopped tomatoes, canned chickpeas (garbanzo beans) and some frozen and fresh produce available. You'll be surprised with what you can create with a few basic ingredients – and it's quicker than waiting for that takeaway!

- **You know the saying: fail to prepare, and prepare to fail** – but let's face it, we don't all have the time to create a weekly meal plan. Even when we do, life can get in the way and we all still need feeding. For those times when you haven't written a meal plan, use this book to decide what to cook, based on the time you have available. In as little as 10 minutes, you can have a tasty supper on the table.

THE SPEEDY STORE CUPBOARD AND FUSS-FREE FRIDGE

Cooking is quick and easy when you have a few speedy staples in your store cupboard. Simple shortcuts can save a whole lot of time, so you can get that supper on the table faster than you think.

CURRY PASTES AND SPICE BLENDS

Spice mix blends such as chilli powder and Chinese five-spice have been blended to create the perfect flavours – all in one jar – meaning that you can have ready-to-use spice blends taking up less room in your cupboard, with minimal fuss when cooking. Ensure curry pastes are vegan-friendly as they can sometimes contain fish sauce or milk. A medium-strength curry paste and a Thai green curry paste are excellent staples to have available.

Speedy Tip

If you're worried about not using up that jar of curry paste, fill ice-cube trays with the paste and freeze. Simply pop one of the frozen curry paste cubes directly into the pan for all the flavour, without any waste.

CANNED BEANS AND PULSES

Beans and pulses are a great source of protein, as well as being a delicious and hearty meal. Canned beans and pulses require no pre-soaking or hours of cooking; simply drain away the liquid and rinse thoroughly in water before adding to your pan or dish, for fuss-free dinners. Look out for no-soak dried red lentils which are quick to cook, and will keep well in your store cupboard.

Speedy Tip

Canned chickpeas (garbanzo beans), butterbeans, red kidney beans, cannellini beans, black beans and green lentils are versatile for a variety of quick meals, as well as being readily available in supermarkets.

PASTA AND NOODLES

Dried pasta is easy to store, and cooks in 10 minutes for a fast dinner. When choosing pasta or noodles, avoid those found in the chiller section of supermarkets, as they are likely to contain eggs. Instead, look for dried pasta, rice noodles or soft noodle varieties in the ambient section, and always read the label to ensure they contain no animal ingredients.

Easy Tip

Most dried pasta available in supermarkets is egg-free, as it is simply made of durum wheat, but always check the label before you buy.

CHOPPED TOMATOES, PASSATA AND TOMATO PURÉE (PASTE)

A humble can of chopped tomatoes is the starting base for so many quick dishes, including curries, soups and bolognese. Chopped tomatoes are cheap to buy, easy to store, and have a long shelf life. Passata is chopped tomatoes that have been sieved, creating a smooth and rich sauce, perfect for pasta sauces. Tomato purée (paste) is thick and has a concentrated flavour – use to top pizza or add a quick burst of flavour to chilli.

Easy Tip

When cooking with chopped tomatoes or passata (sieved tomatoes), which can sometimes taste acidic, simply stir in a pinch of sugar to take away any harsh acidity.

COCONUT MILK

Coconut milk is a versatile ingredient, perfect to add creaminess to curries and soups, as well as desserts, without the need for dairy products.

Easy Tip

Choose full-fat canned varieties for the silkiest texture and rich flavour.

OILS

When used for cooking, oil transmits the heat from the pan to the food for faster, more even cooking with no sticking. Simple sunflower oil or light olive oil are excellent for cooking, as they have no overpowering taste, and are versatile for roasting, frying and baking. Save extra virgin olive oil for dressing salads and pasta, as it has a more complex flavour, as well as being a more expensive option.

SALT

Choose good-quality flaked sea salt for an enhanced flavour to your finished dishes, or season with smoked sea salt flakes for extra depth of seasoning. Simply crush between your fingertips and scatter sparingly.

FRESH VEGETABLES

When choosing fresh vegetables that are suitable for quick and easy dishes, consider ones that are versatile enough to be cooked in a variety of ways. Good examples are carrot, which can grated and used raw, or cooked in a variety of dishes, and spinach, which can be thrown into a stir fry, eaten as a salad leaf, or added to a curry. Quick-cooking vegetables include (bell) peppers, kale, carrots, celery, spring onions (scallions), tomatoes, mushrooms and courgettes (zucchini). When you're in a hurry, consider pre-prepared vegetables such as vacuum-packed beetroot (beet), or peeled and chopped butternut squash, which will save you additional kitchen time. Eat seasonally, for the best quality and price, and with the ever-changing availability of produce, you'll be able to try new things each season. Fresh herbs are a quick way to elevate your dish, giving pops of colour and flavour with very little effort.

Speedy Tip

Frozen vegetables are convenient and quick to use, often with no defrosting time, so you can throw them into the pan and allow them to cook through with the other ingredients. Consider frozen sweetcorn, butternut squash, edamame beans and peas for waste-free options that require very little preparation.

FRESH FRUITS

Soft fruits such as berries, peaches, nectarines, bananas and kiwis are all easy to prepare and versatile enough to be eaten alone, or cooked into a delicious breakfast or dessert. Pomegranate works well in sweet dishes, but is also wonderful in savoury suppers as a colourful and fruity topping; when you're short on time, consider using prepared pomegranate seeds that are available in supermarket chillers.

Speedy Tip

A great way to add extra flavour and freshness to a variety of dishes is to squeeze over some fresh lemon or lime juice. Ensure that the lemons, limes and all citrus fruits are unwaxed, as they can often be waxed with a substance derived from animal products, making them unsuitable for vegans.

TOFU

Long gone are the days of pressing tofu for hours to remove the excess moisture; pre-pressed extra-firm tofu is now available from most supermarkets. Simply blot away any excess moisture, slice as required by the recipe, and cook! (If you don't have pre-pressed tofu, wrap the block in kitchen paper or a clean, dry tea towel and place on a large plate. Place another plate on top of the block and add a couple of cookbooks or a heavy pan over to weigh it down. Allow to stand for 1–2 hours, before slicing the tofu.) Silken tofu is softer, and is best used for desserts and silky sauces.

SHOP-BOUGHT PASTRY

Shop-bought pastry is quick and fuss-free to use, and helps you to create something delicious, without the effort and stress of making your own pastry. Many brands of shop-bought shortcrust, puff and filo pastry use vegetable oil instead of non-vegan butter in the production, making these items suitable for vegans. This can vary from brand to brand, so always check the label before you buy. Ready-rolled pastry is the most convenient to use.

NON-DAIRY ITEMS

Keep a stock of non-dairy items available, which are all now readily available in supermarkets. Unsweetened soya milk is versatile and easy to source, but oat or rice milk make good alternatives. Thick, coconut-based yogurt is delicious to enjoy on its own, but is also wonderful for stirring through savoury dishes for extra richness. Soya- or oat-based pouring creams are delicious and easy to use in the same way a dairy product would be used. Vegan cheeses are widely available to purchase, and have greatly improved in quality over the last few years. Choose your favourite vegan hard and cream cheese, for versatility in cooking – and for snacking!

10

MINUTES

PINEAPPLE & GINGER SMOOTHIE

SERVES 1

I love to wake up with this fresh smoothie, which is packed with energy and goodness for the morning ahead. The ginger is warming and packs a spicy punch! Add more or less water depending on how thick you enjoy your smoothies.

2 tbsp frozen pineapple

2cm (¾in) piece of ginger, peeled

1 banana, peeled

handful of fresh spinach leaves

1 Add the frozen pineapple, ginger, banana and spinach to a high-powered blender jug, then pour in 100ml (scant ½ cup) cold water.

2 Blitz until completely smooth, adding a little extra water if desired to make your perfect smoothie consistency.

Speedy Tip

Prepare the ingredients the evening before and keep refrigerated in a jar. The frozen pineapple will thaw, so add a little less water when blending. Frozen pineapple is readily available in supermarkets, or feel free to use fresh pineapple, if you have the time to prepare it.

BREAKFAST BANANA SPLIT

SERVES 2

Dessert for breakfast? Yes please! This morning-friendly twist on the classic dessert will have you jumping out of bed to indulge. Opt for the thick coconut variety of yogurt, with a high coconut cream percentage, for added creaminess and luxury. I love drizzling over some maple syrup, but feel free to mix it up with vegan chocolate sauce. Or serve with sliced mango, for a taste of the tropics.

4 tbsp thick coconut yogurt

2 bananas, peeled and halved lengthways

2 tsp rolled oats

2 tsp toasted flaked coconut

2 tsp blanched and chopped hazelnuts

generous drizzle of maple syrup

1   Dollop 2 tablespoons of coconut yogurt onto each plate, then arrange the bananas on top.

2   Scatter over 1 teaspoon each of oats, desiccated coconut and chopped hazelnuts per plate.

3   Drizzle over maple syrup just before serving.

Speedy Tip
Blanched and chopped hazelnuts can be found in supermarkets, for time-saving ease.

ONE-MINUTE CRANBERRY AND PECAN MUESLI

SERVES 2

There's no excuse not to eat breakfast when this muesli takes just one minute to prepare. Not only is it delicious with the flavours of pecan, cranberries and apple, it is nutritionally balanced to set you up for the day ahead. I love serving this with apple juice poured over, but if you prefer your muesli with plant-based milk, ice-cold almond milk is a delicious substitution.

6 tbsp rolled oats

2 tbsp dried cranberries

2 rounded tbsp pecans, roughly broken or chopped

1 tbsp pumpkin seeds

pinch of ground cinnamon

generous splash of good-quality chilled apple juice, to serve

1   In a large bowl, toss together the oats, cranberries, pecans, pumpkin seeds and ground cinnamon until evenly distributed.

2   Spoon into serving bowls and pour over the apple juice just before serving.

Speedy Tip

Mix the dry ingredients in advance and store in an airtight container. Feel free to double or even triple the recipe to save precious morning time.

MARMALADE MICROWAVE PORRIDGE

SERVES 1

Want the comfort of porridge without waiting for the simmer of a pan?
This creamy porridge is perfect from the microwave, with a hint of nutmeg
and a spoonful of tangy sweet orange marmalade. You won't look back!

3 tbsp rolled oats

pinch of grated nutmeg

200ml (generous ¾ cup) almond milk, plus 2 tbsp for stirring in

2 tsp golden raisins

1 tbsp good-quality orange marmalade

1 In a heatproof bowl, stir together the oats, nutmeg and the almond milk.

2 Cook in the microwave on high for 2 minutes, then stir and cook for 1 further minute.

3 Carefully remove from the microwave and stir in the extra almond milk, to loosen and cool the porridge a little. Stir in the sultanas and top with a dollop of marmalade.

Speedy Tip

The perfect consistency of porridge is a personal thing, isn't it? Feel free to add more or less almond milk after cooking to loosen the texture.

CREAM CHEESE, POPPY SEED AND CUCUMBER TOAST

SERVES 2

Hot toasted sourdough, cooling cream cheese, crunchy poppy seeds and fresh cucumber are brought together with flavoursome chives for a light yet satisfying breakfast. If you can get hold of mini cucumbers, their petite slices make a fun and pretty alternative to larger slices of cucumber.

2 thick slices of sourdough bread

2 tbsp vegan cream cheese

pinch of poppy seeds

6 chives, chopped

4cm (I½in) piece of cucumber, thinly sliced

pinch of sea salt

1   Toast the slices of bread under a grill (broiler) or in a toaster until lightly golden.

2   When the bread is toasted, generously smooth over the cream cheese and sprinkle with poppy seeds and half of the chopped chives.

3   Lay over the cucumber slices and scatter with the remaining chives. Season to taste with a pinch of sea salt.

Speedy Tip

Save time by slicing the cucumbers and chopping the chives while the bread is toasting.

FROZEN YOGURT BARK

SERVES 2

Take 10 minutes out of your evening to prepare a breakfast perfect for a summer's morning. This yogurt bark does take some time to set in the freezer, but the preparation is quick and the results are worth it! I love the tropical flavours of banana and kiwi in this bark, but feel free to use seasonal berries or cherries.

500g (1lb 2oz) soya yogurt

2 generous tbsp maple syrup

2 tbsp desiccated (dried shredded) coconut

1 tbsp dried cranberries

1 small banana, peeled and thinly sliced

1 kiwi, peeled and slcied lengthways into chunks

2 tbsp toasted flaked coconut

1 Line a large baking tray with foil.

2 In a bowl, stir together the soya yogurt and maple syrup until combined, then stir in 1 tbsp desiccated coconut.

3 Spread the yogurt mixture on the lined baking tray, so it is just a couple of millimetres thick. Place the sliced banana, chopped kiwi and cranberries over the top, then scatter with the remaining desiccated coconut and the toasted flaked coconut. Ensure all the toppings are pushed into the yogurt slightly.

4 Freeze overnight or for at least 4 hours until solid. Snap into roughly shaped and sized pieces, or cut with a sharp knife.

Speedy Tip

After the yogurt bark has frozen, snap it into pieces and return whatever you don't eat to the freezer in a freezer-safe container.

CHICKPEA, CARROT AND OLIVE SALAD

SERVES 2 GENEROUSLY

This speedy salad can be thrown together with store cupboard staples and just a few fresh ingredients for a flavoursome lunch – perfect for al fresco summer days. It's worth spending a couple of minutes toasting the pine nuts while you prepare the rest of the salad, to bring out the nutty flavour.

2 tsp pine nuts

1 x 400g (14oz) can of chickpeas (garbanzo beans), drained and rinsed

2 carrots, peeled and grated

8 black olives, pitted

6 dried apricots, roughly chopped

generous handful of flat-leaf parsley, finely chopped

4 mint leaves, finely chopped

juice of ½ unwaxed lemon

drizzle of extra virgin olive oil

generous pinch of sea salt

1   Toast the pine nuts in a dry pan over a medium-high heat for 2–3 minutes until fragrant.

2   In a bowl, stir together the chickpeas, carrots, olives, apricots, chopped parsley and mint.

3   Stir through the lemon juice and olive oil, then stir through the toasted pine nuts. Season to taste with sea salt.

Speedy Tip

This salad will last well when refrigerated for up to 3 days, making it the perfect lunch for batch preparation.

LEMON, DILL AND BUTTERBEAN DIP

SERVES 2

Looking for a quick and easy dip for lunch? Look no further than this fresh and creamy lemon and butterbean dip. Serve with your favourite crudités, including carrot sticks, celery, apple wedges, red pepper, radishes, mini cucumbers and figs, or spread on thick, toasted bread. The dip will last for up to 3 days in a sealed container in the fridge.

1 x 400g (14oz) can or jar of butterbeans, drained and rinsed

juice of ½ unwaxed lemon

1 tbsp extra virgin olive oil

pinch of sea salt

generous handful of dill, finely chopped

small handful of flat-leaf parsley, finely chopped

1 Add the butterbeans, lemon juice, olive oil and sea salt to a blender jug and blitz until smooth.

2 Stir through the dill and parsley until evenly distributed.

Speedy Tip

If you prefer a chunkier dip, simply use a fork to roughly mash the butterbeans instead of blitzing in a blender.

MEXICAN-STYLE STREET CORN

SERVES 2

Traditionally, Mexican street corn is grilled on a barbecue before being smothered in a smoky mayonnaise. I don't know about you, but I have little inclination to fire up the barbecue over lunch time, so I adapted this recipe so you can simmer the corn on the cobs in a pan until tender and milky. Then simply spoon over the creamy dressing – for a fun and fresh lunch ready in just 10 minutes.

4 corn on the cob, husks removed

1 tsp sugar

3 rounded tbsp vegan mayonnaise, chilled

1 tbsp barbecue sauce (ensure vegan)

pinch of smoked paprika

pinch of dried chilli flakes

2 spring onions (scallions), finely chopped

small handful of coriander (cilantro) leaves, finely chopped

squeeze of juice from an unwaxed lime

generous pinch of smoked sea salt

1   Bring a large pan of water to the boil over a medium-high heat. Carefully add the corn cobs and the sugar. Boil for 7–8 minutes, or until tender.

2   Meanwhile, add the mayonnaise, barbecue sauce, smoked paprika and chilli flakes to a bowl and stir to combine. Mix in the spring onions and chopped coriander, then stir through the lime juice and season to taste with smoked sea salt.

3   Remove the pan from the heat and drain away the water. Place the corn cobs on a chopping board and spoon over the smoky mayonnaise, smoothing it down the sides. Serve hot.

Speedy Tip

For an even speedier version of this lunch, make a salad using drained and rinsed cans of sweetcorn, with the mayonnaise stirred through. Serve with fresh salad leaves and warmed tortillas, if you like.

LUNCHTIME LOADED NACHOS

SERVES 2

Nachos for lunch? Of course! These home-baked tortilla chips are loaded with all the good stuff that you'd normally find on a salad (but it's much more fun to eat when it's over crispy nachos!). Prepare the vegetables while you wait for the nachos to cook, to save precious time.

2 large soft white tortilla wraps, sliced into small triangles

drizzle of sunflower oil

pinch of dried chilli flakes

30g (1oz) hard vegan cheese, grated

6 pitted black olives, roughly sliced into rings

2 spring onions (scallions), finely chopped

1 yellow (bell) pepper, finely diced

2 cherry tomatoes, quartered

1 avocado, diced

200g (7oz) canned red kidney beans, drained and rinsed

generous pinch of sea salt

1 Preheat the oven to 190°C/375°F/gas mark 5.

2 Lay the tortilla triangles on a large baking tray (or two smaller ones) so they do not overlap. Use a pastry brush to sweep them with the oil, then sprinkle with chilli flakes. Bake in the oven for 5–6 minutes until lightly golden.

3 Remove from the oven and scatter with the grated cheese. Carefully return the tray to the oven and cook for a further 2–3 minutes until the cheese has melted.

4 Remove the tray from the oven and scoop the cheesy nachos into bowls. Scatter with olives, spring onions, pepper, tomatoes, avocado and kidney beans, then season with sea salt.

Speedy Tip

You'll find small (200g/7oz) cans of red kidney beans available in large supermarkets, which provide the perfect amount for this lunch. Alternatively, use half a standard size can (400g/14oz) and freeze the remainder in a container for next time.

CREAMY PEA SOUP WITH MINT AND LEMON

SERVES 4 · SUITABLE FOR FREEZING

All the comfort of creamy soup – in just 10 minutes. Whether you're working from home, taking a jar of soup to the office, or filling a flask for a picnic, this soup is full of flavour and freshness. Put those frozen peas to good use! Substitute soya cream for oat cream or vegan crème fraîche, if you prefer. All of these options are available in most supermarkets.

I tbsp sunflower oil

I onion, finely chopped

I garlic clove, crushed

300g (10oz) frozen peas

800ml (3⅓ cups) hot vegetable stock

handful of mint leaves, finely chopped

small handful of flat-leaf parsley, finely chopped

juice of ½ unwaxed lemon

generous pinch of sea salt and black pepper

4 tbsp single (light) soya cream

1   Heat the oil in a large pan, add the onion and garlic and cook over a high heat for 1 minute until fragrant.

2   Pour in the frozen peas and vegetable stock, then loosely cover with the pan lid. Boil for 7 minutes, then carefully pour or ladle into a high-powered blender jug. Blitz on high until completely smooth.

3   Stir in the chopped mint and parsley, reserving a small handful to serve, then squeeze in the lemon juice. Season to taste with plenty of salt and pepper. Ladle into bowls and drizzle over the soya cream just before serving. Top with the reserved herbs and plenty of black pepper.

Speedy Tip

Save time by chopping the fresh herbs while the pan is simmering, then stir them in after the soup has been blitzed smooth.

BUTTERNUT SQUASH, SAGE AND CARAMELIZED ONION TOASTIE

SERVES 2

Diced and frozen butternut squash (found in most supermarkets) is a revelation. Not only is it easy to prepare without the tricky peeling, but it cooks in minutes, making it the perfect ingredient for this autumn-inspired toastie. Combine butternut squash, sage and a dash of maple syrup to make a comforting and chunky spread, then sandwich together with caramelized onion chutney before toasting, for the ultimate rainy day lunch.

200g (7oz) frozen butternut squash

¼ tsp dried sage

I tsp maple syrup

generous pinch of sea salt and black pepper

4 thick slices of white bread

2 tsp vegan butter

2 tbsp caramelized onion chutney

1 Bring a pan of water to the boil over a medium-high heat, then add the frozen butternut squash. Boil for 3–4 minutes until tender, then thoroughly drain away the water.

2 Transfer the cooked butternut squash to a bowl and use a fork to mash it into a chunky spread. Stir in the sage and maple syrup, then season with salt and pepper.

3 Lay out the slices of bread on a clean work surface and butter both sides of each slice. Spread the butternut squash mix generously on two slices of bread, then spoon on some caramelized onion chutney. Top the sandwiches with the remaining slices of bread.

4 Place a large, dry frying pan over a high heat and carefully place the sandwiches in using a metal spatula. Gently press down and cook for 2 minutes until golden before flipping the sandwiches and cooking the remaining side for a further 2 minutes.

5 Carefully remove from the pan and slice before serving hot.

Speedy Tip

The butternut squash and sage spread will keep for up to 3 days in the fridge in a sealed container, and is also suitable for freezing, making your next toastie extra quick and easy!

BLOOD ORANGE, RED CABBAGE AND LENTIL SALAD

SERVES 2 GENEROUSLY

This salad delivers on style, flavour and substance – and it's very easy to put together with no cooking involved. It works well for batch preparation, and is delicious as a lunch, jacket potato filling, or as a lighter side dish for a main meal.

1 blood orange, peeled and thinly sliced

1 red cabbage, finely shredded

1 carrot, peeled and grated

1 x 400g (14oz) can of green or brown lentils, drained and rinsed

seeds of 1 pomegranate (about 200g/7oz)

2 tbsp shelled pistachios, roughly chopped

4 tbsp extra virgin olive oil

squeeze of juice from an unwaxed lemon

small handful of flat-leaf parsley, finely chopped

pinch of sea salt and black pepper

1 In a large bowl, combine the orange slices, cabbage, carrot, lentils, pomegranate seeds and pistachios.

2 In a jug, whisk together the olive oil, lemon juice and chopped parsley, then season to taste with salt and pepper.

3 Stir the dressing through the salad until evenly distributed.

Speedy Tip

Buy pomegranate seeds instead of a whole pomegranate, and shelled pistachios, to save time (and reduce mess in the kitchen).

CHINESE-STYLE HOT AND SOUR BROTH WITH TOFU

SERVES 4 GENEROUSLY · SUITABLE FOR FREEZING

Sometimes lunchtime calls for a glossy, brothy bowl of flavour and goodness.
I love the tangy, spicy and savoury broth surrounding cubes of tofu,
beansprouts and crunchy water chestnuts. I always have some of this
in the freezer, for busy days when I need a light lunch – fast.

1 tbsp sunflower oil

1 carrot, peeled and sliced into half-rounds

6 button mushrooms, halved

2 spring onions (scallions), thinly sliced into shreds

½ small red chilli, deseeded and thinly sliced

2 garlic cloves, crushed

1 litre (4 cups) hot vegetable stock

150g (5oz) beansprouts

1 x 225g (8oz) can of water chestnuts, thoroughly drained and rinsed

1 tbsp tomato purée (paste)

100g (3½oz) extra-firm tofu, drained and blotted then cut into chunks

1 tbsp malt vinegar

1 tbsp dark soy sauce

handful of chives, chopped

handful of coriander (cilantro), roughly chopped

1 Heat the oil in a large wok over a high heat, then throw in the carrot, mushrooms, most of the spring onions and the chilli. Stir-fry for 1 minute, then add the garlic and stir until evenly distributed.

2 Pour in the stock and add the beansprouts, water chestnuts, tomato purée and tofu. Cook for 8 minutes, stirring occasionally to prevent sticking or boiling over.

3 Remove the pan from the heat and stir through the vinegar and soy sauce. Scatter with chives, coriander and remaining spring onions just before serving.

Speedy Tip

There's no need to press or pre-cook the tofu. Simply remove from the package, blot any excess moisture away with kitchen paper or a clean tea towel, then chop for melt-in-the-mouth texture once cooked in the broth.

EGG-LESS AND WATERCRESS SANDWICHES

SERVES 4

These sandwiches will ignite memories of childhood lunches past, without the animal ingredients! Opt for a pre-pressed extra-firm tofu (found in supermarkets) to save hours of pressing time – plus there's no need to cook the tofu as the texture perfectly substitutes hard-boiled eggs. Don't skip the mustard or chives; they lift the flavour for that authentic lunchtime classic. If you can source kala namak, or black salt, it gives an added 'egg' flavour to the mix, but it's not essential as the dressing will work just as beautifully with sea salt.

5 rounded tbsp vegan mayonnaise

½ tsp Dijon mustard

pinch of ground turmeric

handful of chives, finely chopped

generous pinch of sea salt, or black salt (kala namak)

1 x 400g (14oz) can of cannellini beans, drained and rinsed

250g (9oz) extra-firm tofu, drained and blotted

wedge of lemon, for squeezing

8 thick slices of white bread

4 tsp vegan butter

¼ cucumber, peeled and thinly sliced

2 handfuls of watercress

1   In a bowl, stir together the mayonnaise, mustard, turmeric, chives and salt until combined.

2   Add the cannellini beans to a food processor and blitz until roughly crushed, or use a fork to crush them in a bowl. Stir the crushed beans into the mayonnaise mix.

3   Roughly crumble in the tofu, leaving some chunks larger than others, then stir to coat the crumbled tofu in the mayonnaise and bean mixture. Squeeze in a little lemon juice then allow to stand for a few minutes to infuse.

4   Lay out the bread on a clean work surface and butter each slice. Generously load in the egg-less filling and smooth down before topping with some cucumber and watercress. Finish with the remaining bread slices then slice to your preference.

Speedy Tip

If you don't use all of the sandwich filling, it can be kept for up to 2 days in the fridge in a sealed container.

TAGLIATELLE WITH CAVOLO NERO, CHILLI, GARLIC AND LEMON

SERVES 2

This 10-minute meal is a regular in my kitchen. It's simple, filling, satisfying and comforting, with just a few ingredients. Don't miss out the chilli flakes or lemon juice; they lift what would be a basic dish to another level.

6–8 nests of dried tagliatelle (ensure egg-free)

generous drizzle of olive oil

6 large leaves of cavolo nero, roughly sliced, tough stalks removed and discarded

pinch of dried chilli flakes

2 garlic cloves, thinly sliced

juice of ½ unwaxed lemon

generous pinch of sea salt and black pepper

1   Bring a large pan of water to the boil over a high heat and drop in the tagliatelle. Cook for 8–10 minutes until al dente.

2   Meanwhile, in a separate flat pan, drizzle in the olive oil and scatter in the cavolo nero and chilli flakes. Cook over a medium heat for 5 minutes until the leaves have softened and become brighter in colour. Add the garlic and cook for a further 1–2 minutes until fragrant.

3   Thoroughly drain the water from the pasta, then stir through the cooked cavolo nero mixture, including any remaining cooking oil. Squeeze over the lemon juice and season generously with salt and pepper.

Speedy Tip

Many brands of dried tagliatelle are egg-free as they simply use semolina flour. Always check the ingredients, and avoid the refrigerated 'fresh' pasta which is likely to contain eggs.

GARLIC BROCCOLI WITH CASHEWS

SERVES 2 · SUITABLE FOR FREEZING

Treat yourself to a classic Chinese takeaway-style meal, any night of the week, in under 10 minutes. Serve with some quick-cook basmati rice, or spread the meal further by enjoying with special fried rice (overleaf).

1 tbsp sunflower oil

1 medium head of broccoli, chopped into bite-sized florets

2cm (¾in) piece of ginger, grated

1 garlic clove, crushed

pinch of dried chilli flakes

pinch of Chinese five-spice

1 tbsp light soy sauce

4 rounded tbsp roasted cashews

2 spring onions (scallions), finely chopped

sweet chilli sauce, to serve (ensure vegan)

1 Heat the oil in a wok over a high heat, then throw in the broccoli. Stir-fry for 1 minute until the broccoli appears bright in colour.

2 Add the ginger, garlic, chilli flakes and Chinese five-spice and stir-fry for a further minute.

3 Stir in the soy sauce and cashews and stir-fry for 2–3 minutes until the broccoli is tender.

4 Remove from the heat and scatter with spring onions just before serving with some sweet chilli sauce on the side.

Speedy Tip

Store peeled fresh ginger in the freezer, then simply grate from frozen into the wok.

SPECIAL FRIED RICE

SERVES 2

Fried rice works best when using rice that has been pre-cooked a few hours in advance – or the day before – and kept in the fridge (make sure you cool cooked rice completely before refrigerating). If you meal-plan, cook a little extra rice with your normal amount and whip up this speedy meal the following day. This is a complete (and filling) dish, or serve as a side to garlic broccoli with cashews (page 52).

2 tbsp sunflower oil

2 spring onions (scallions), finely chopped

2cm (¾in) piece of ginger, grated

1 garlic clove, crushed

pinch of dried chilli flakes

pinch of Chinese five-spice

1 carrot, peeled and thinly sliced into half-rounds

10 sugarsnap peas, diagonally sliced in half

2 tbsp cashews

2 tbsp frozen or fresh podded edamame beans

1 tbsp frozen peas

200g (7oz) cooked basmati rice

2 tbsp dark soy sauce

juice of ½ unwaxed lime

small handful of coriander (cilantro) leaves, roughly torn

1   Heat the oil in a wok over a high heat, then throw in the spring onions, ginger, garlic, chilli flakes and Chinese five-spice. Stir-fry for up to a minute until fragrant.

2   Add the carrot, sugarsnap peas, cashews, edamame beans and peas and stir-fry for 2 minutes.

3   Add the cooked rice and soy sauce then stir-fry for a further 2 minutes, to distribute the sauce evenly through the rice and vegetables.

4   Remove from the heat and stir in the lime juice. Scatter with coriander just before serving.

Speedy Tip

Cooked rice pouches are available in supermarkets and are a speedy and convenient alternative to pre-cooking the rice at home; they give excellent results in this dish.

Pictured on page 53.

CRISPY AIR FRYER SALT AND PEPPER TOFU

SERVES 2

One of my favourite ways to cook tofu is in an air fryer (it's not just for chips!), as it is crispy on the outside and tender on the inside, without soaking up excess oil from deep-frying. Depending on the size of your air fryer, you may have to adjust the cooking time to within a couple of minutes, because the more you can space out the tofu, the faster it will cook and crisp up. Of course, if you don't have an air fryer, deep-frying the tofu for 4–5 minutes is a good alternative. Opt for a pre-pressed extra-firm tofu, to save hours of preparation time. Serve with steamed broccoli and rice, and a drizzle of dark soy sauce.

1 tsp cornflour (cornstarch)

¼ tsp Chinese five-spice

generous pinch of sea salt

280g (10oz) extra-firm tofu, drained and blotted, cut into bite-sized chunks

1 tbsp plus 2 tsp sunflower oil

3 spring onions (scallions), finely sliced

1 red chilli, deseeded and thinly sliced into rounds

2 garlic cloves, thinly sliced

1cm (½in) piece of ginger, grated

1   Preheat the air fryer to 200°C/400°F.

2   Spoon the cornflour, Chinese five-spice and salt into a large, clean, food-safe bag. Shake to combine. Add the tofu chunks to the bag and shake vigorously to coat.

3   Add the coated tofu to the air fryer basket rack, in a single layer if possible (you may have to do this in two batches depending on the size of the air fryer model). Drizzle with the 2 teaspoons of sunflower oil and shake, then cook for 7–8 minutes until golden, shaking the basket halfway through.

4   Meanwhile, heat the 1 tablespoon of sunflower oil in a wok over a high heat. Add the spring onions, chilli, garlic and ginger and stir-fry for 1–2 minutes until softened and fragrant.

5   Remove the cooked tofu from the air fryer and allow it to rest for a moment. Place the tofu in a serving bowl then spoon over the cooked spring onions, chilli, garlic and ginger.

Speedy Tip

I find that shaking the tofu in a food-safe bag with the dry ingredients is the best way of coating the tofu chunks, but if you don't have a bag large enough to do this, add the cornflour, Chinese five-spice and salt to a bowl, then sift this over the tofu to give a light dusting, turning the tofu halfway.

Pictured on page 53.

GOLDEN PANCAKES WITH SWEETCORN SALSA

SERVES 4

If you're looking for a time-saving midweek meal, these pancakes are fun, fast and use store cupboard ingredients. The sweetcorn salsa is versatile enough to use as a jacket potato filling, as a side for chilli, or as a quick salad for lunch. If you prefer a little heat, slice a red chilli into the sweetcorn salsa, or keep it mild for a family-friendly salsa.

For the savoury pancakes

100g (scant 1 cup) plain (all-purpose) flour

pinch of ground turmeric

generous pinch of sea salt

200ml (generous ¾ cup) soya milk, chilled

6 tbsp sunflower oil, for frying

For the sweetcorn salsa

3 x 198g (7oz) cans of sweetcorn, drained and rinsed

1 red (bell) pepper, finely diced

4 spring onions (scallions), finely sliced

2 ripe tomatoes, deseeded and finely diced

handful of coriander (cilantro), finely chopped

small handful of flat-leaf parsley, finely chopped

juice of 1 unwaxed lime, plus wedges (optional) for serving

generous pinch of smoked sea salt flakes

1 To make the pancakes, stir together the flour, turmeric and salt. Whisk in the soya milk until you have a smooth batter with no lumps. Allow the batter to rest for a few moments.

2 Heat 1 tbsp oil in a flat frying pan over a medium-high heat. Use a ladle to add batter to the pan, smooth over and cook for 1–2 minutes before flipping and cooking the other side. Repeat with the remaining oil and batter. Keep the pancakes warm.

3 In a bowl, combine the sweetcorn, red pepper, spring onions, tomatoes, coriander and parsley. Squeeze over the lime juice and season with smoked sea salt.

4 Load the salsa into each pancake and fold over. Serve with a wedge of lime, if you wish.

Speedy Tip

Make the pancake batter up to a day in advance and keep refrigerated. It will naturally thicken during this time, so whisk in a little soya milk to loosen to a pouring consistency.

CREAMY TUSCAN BEANS

SERVES 2 GENEROUSLY · SUITABLE FOR FREEZING

This one-pot delight is creamy and comforting, with bursts of Italian flavour from tomatoes, vegan cheese and basil. Serve with toast, freshly steamed greens, or with flat ribbon pasta.

1 tbsp sunflower oil

1 onion, finely chopped

3 garlic cloves, crushed

10 fine green beans, trimmed and halved

6 cherry tomatoes, halved

1 tsp dried oregano

pinch of dried mixed herbs

250ml (1 cup) dairy-free double (heavy) cream

1 tbsp vegan cream cheese

1 x 400g (14oz) can of cannellini beans, drained and rinsed

2 generous handfuls of spinach leaves

6 sundried tomatoes in oil, drained and roughly sliced

generous pinch of sea salt and black pepper

handful of small basil leaves

1 Heat the oil in a large pan and add the onion, garlic, green beans and cherry tomatoes. Cook over a medium-high heat for 2 minutes until they begin to soften. Stir in the oregano and mixed herbs.

2 Stir in the cream, cream cheese and cannellini beans, then simmer for 5 minutes, stirring frequently.

3 Add the spinach and sundried tomatoes, then cook for a further 3 minutes until the spinach has wilted. Season to taste with salt and plenty of pepper, then scatter with basil leaves just before serving.

Speedy Tip

You'll find dairy-free double (heavy) cream available in most supermarkets. It has a thick and smooth mouthfeel, similar to that of its dairy counterpart.

PAPRIKA CHICKPEAS WITH PARSLEY AND LEMON

SERVES 2 GENEROUSLY · SUITABLE FOR FREEZING

Hearty, full of flavour, and a comforting crowd-pleaser, no one will believe that this meal is ready in just 10 minutes. Serve with warmed, crusty bread and olive oil.

1 tbsp sunflower oil

1 onion, finely diced

2 garlic cloves, sliced

1 yellow (bell) pepper, thinly sliced

2 rounded tsp smoked paprika

pinch of dried chilli flakes

1 x 400g (14oz) can of good-quality chopped tomatoes

1 x 400g (14oz) can of chickpeas (garbanzo beans), drained and rinsed

pinch of granulated sugar

1 sprig of fresh thyme

10 black olives, pitted

2 handfuls of spinach leaves

generous handful of flat-leaf parsley, finely chopped

juice of ½ unwaxed lemon

generous pinch of sea salt flakes

1 Heat the oil in a large pan, add the onion, garlic and sliced pepper and cook for 1 minute over a medium-high heat until they begin to soften.

2 Stir in the smoked paprika and chilli flakes until the vegetables are coated, then pour in the chopped tomatoes, chickpeas and pinch of sugar. Place in the sprig of thyme, then cook over a high heat for 7 minutes, stirring frequently to avoid sticking.

3 Stir in the olives and spinach and cook for a further minute.

4 Remove from the heat and stir through the parsley. Squeeze over the lemon juice and season to taste with salt.

Speedy Tip

If you happen to have any leftovers, stir in some hot vegetable stock and enjoy a chunky soup for lunch the following day.

EVERYTHING TOMATO SAUCE

MAKES AROUND 6 PORTIONS · SUITABLE FOR FREEZING

One sauce, many dishes. Make up a batch of this sauce to pour over pasta, use as a base for bolognese, lasagne, ratatouille, minestrone soup, or as a pizza sauce. Spoon into freezer-safe containers and freeze until needed – for when you want a meal without the fuss. It's also easy to double up the recipe.

drizzle of sunflower oil

2 garlic cloves, crushed

800g (3½ cups/1lb 12oz) good-quality passata (sieved tomatoes)

pinch of granulated sugar

generous handful of basil leaves, finely chopped

small handful of flat-leaf parsley, finely chopped

generous pinch of sea salt and black pepper

1   Heat the oil in a large pan, add the garlic and cook over a medium heat for 1 minute until fragrant.

2   Pour in the passata, along with 100ml (scant ½ cup) of water, and stir in the sugar. Cover the pan loosely with a lid, then simmer for 10 minutes, stirring occasionally.

3   Remove from the heat and stir through the basil and parsley. Season to taste with salt and pepper.

Speedy Tip

To defrost, simply remove from the freezer and leave at room temperature for 6–8 hours.

COURGETTE AND RED PEPPER PIZZA BAGUETTES

SERVES 2

All the pizza experience, with none of the extra effort – sounds like the perfect Friday night supper to me! These pizzas are made using baguettes for a perfect bready base; I like to use tiger baguettes, but sourdough and seeded varieties are delicious too. Slice the courgette thinly for a super-speedy roasting time.

2 white baguettes (French sticks), sliced in half lengthways

4 tbsp tomato purée (paste)

8 thin rounds of courgette (zucchini), cut into semicircles

½ red (bell) pepper, thinly sliced

½ small red onion, thinly sliced

4 cherry tomatoes, halved

4 button mushrooms, sliced

generous pinch of dried oregano

drizzle of extra virgin olive oil

pinch of sea salt and black pepper

generous handful of rocket (arugula) leaves

1   Preheat the oven to 200°C/400°F/gas mark 6.

2   Lay out the sliced baguettes and smooth over 1 tablespoon of tomato purée per half baguette.

3   Place the baguettes on a baking tray (it's easier than lifting them over once the toppings are on!) and arrange the sliced courgette, pepper, onion, tomatoes and mushrooms over the top of each baguette half.

4   Sprinkle over the oregano and drizzle with olive oil. Bake in the oven for 8 minutes until the edges are golden and the toppings are hot.

5   Remove from the oven and season with salt and pepper. Top with the rocket leaves and drizzle with more extra virgin olive oil, if you like.

Speedy Tip

Squeeze the leftover tomato purée into ice-cube trays and freeze to prevent waste. Simply pop the frozen tomato purée directly into dishes such as coconut chana masala (page 70) or defrost to use on pizzas.

CAPONATA GNOCCHI

SERVES 2 GENEROUSLY · SUITABLE FOR FREEZING

Two pans, ten minutes, ultimate comfort food. Combine two Italian classics in this quick and flavoursome supper that everyone will love. Prepare for this dish to become a week-night staple in your kitchen!

2 tbsp sunflower oil

1 aubergine (eggplant), chopped into 3cm (1in) cubes

1 tsp dried oregano

1 red onion, thinly sliced

1 garlic clove, thinly sliced

8 cherry tomatoes

1 tbsp sultanas (golden raisins)

1 tbsp balsamic vinegar

10 green olives, pitted and halved

500g (1lb 2oz) gnocchi (ensure dairy- and egg-free)

juice of ¼ unwaxed lemon

pinch of sea salt and black pepper

generous handful of basil leaves

1   Heat 1 tablespoon of the oil in a large frying pan over a high heat and cook the aubergine, oregano and red onion for 5 minutes until the aubergine starts to soften.

2   Add the garlic, cherry tomatoes, sultanas, balsamic vinegar and olives to the pan. Stir through and cook for 4 minutes over a medium-high heat.

3   Meanwhile, bring a large pan of water to the boil. Add the gnocchi and cook for 3–4 minutes until softened, then drain thoroughly.

4   Remove the frying pan from the heat. Stir in the cooked gnocchi, lemon juice, salt and pepper until the gnocchi is coated. Scatter with basil leaves just before serving.

Speedy Tip

Shop-bought potato gnocchi is a store cupboard essential which is quick to cook and comforting to eat with a delicious sauce. Many brands are dairy- and egg-free, but always check the ingredients before you buy.

SPICY PEANUT STIR FRY WITH NOODLES

SERVES 2

Take simple stir fry and noodles to the next level with a rich peanut sauce, chilli, ginger, lime and sesame seeds. I love the combination of vegetables used in this recipe as they are fast to prepare, but feel free to add in any extras you have available.

2 rounded tbsp smooth peanut butter

1 tbsp dark soy sauce

1 tbsp sunflower oil

2cm (¾in) piece of ginger, grated

pinch of dried chilli flakes

1 carrot, peeled and thinly sliced

6 sugarsnap peas, sliced lengthways

4 baby corns, roughly chopped

2 x 150g (5oz) packs of soft noodles (ensure egg-free)

2 spring onions (scallions), finely sliced

1 tbsp roasted and salted peanuts, finely chopped

2 tsp sesame seeds

squeeze of juice from an unwaxed lime

handful of coriander (cilantro) leaves, roughly torn

1   Spoon the peanut butter and soy sauce into a jug or bowl then pour in 200ml (generous ¾ cup) boiling water. Use a balloon whisk to combine until creamy, then set aside.

2   Heat the oil in a large wok over a high heat, then add the ginger, chilli flakes, carrot, sugarsnaps and baby corns and stir-fry for 2 minutes.

3   Add the noodles and stir, then pour in the peanut butter mixture. Stir-fry for 4–5 minutes until the noodles and vegetables are coated and the sauce has thickened.

4   Remove from the heat and scatter with spring onions, chopped peanuts and sesame seeds. Stir in the lime juice and coriander leaves just before serving.

Speedy Tip

Soft noodles are a store cupboard staple, but do make sure they are vegan. Many types found in the chiller section will contain eggs, so look to the ambient aisles for egg-free soft noodles as they are less likely to contain animal ingredients. If you find that the noodles stick together in the pack, simply soak them in a bowl of hot water for a couple of minutes before draining and adding to the wok.

SIZZLING PEPPER, RED ONION AND BLACK BEAN FAJITAS

SERVES 4

This crowd-pleasing supper is fresh, fun and filling, with Tex-Mex-inspired flavours and black beans. Feel free to load with tomato salsa and guacamole, or keep it simple with avocado slices and lime juice. I use shop-bought salsa for speediness, but feel free to make your own with tomatoes, red onion, coriander, lime juice and sea salt.

I tbsp sunflower oil

I red (bell) pepper, sliced

I yellow (bell) pepper, sliced

I red onion, thinly sliced

I celery stick, diced

I tsp mild chilli powder

I tsp smoked paprika

pinch of dried thyme

pinch of ground cumin

I x 400g (14oz) can of black beans, drained and rinsed

8 soft white tortilla wraps

I avocado, sliced

4 tsp vegan mayonnaise

generous pinch of sea salt

juice of ½ unwaxed lime

small handful of coriander (cilantro) leaves, roughly torn

1 Heat the sunflower oil in a large frying pan or wok over a medium-high heat. Throw in the peppers, red onion and celery and stir-fry for 3–4 minutes.

2 Sprinkle in the chilli powder, smoked paprika, thyme and cumin and stir-fry for another minute.

3 Stir in the black beans and coat in the spicy vegetable mix until they are heated through, about 2–3 minutes.

4 Meanwhile, warm the tortilla wraps in the oven for a couple of minutes. When they are warmed, lay slices of avocado in each, with a spoonful of mayonnaise.

5 Remove the pan from the heat and season with salt. Stir in the lime juice and scatter over the coriander leaves. Load the mix into the tortilla wraps and serve hot.

Speedy Tip

I love a spoonful of cooling vegan mayonnaise in each fajita, and the slight acidity works well with the spices. Feel free to switch this for dairy-free cream cheese, or plain vegan yogurt if you have them available.

COCONUT CHANA MASALA

SERVES 4 · SUITABLE FOR FREEZING

Traditionally, chana masala is a chickpea curry with a tomato base. I love substituting the chopped tomatoes for creamy coconut milk, for a supper that is just as quick, and doubly delicious. Serve with rice, vegan naan bread and a spoonful of lime pickle to stand up to the creamy sauce. Perfect for batch cooking.

1 tbsp sunflower oil

1 onion, finely diced

2 garlic cloves, crushed

1 tsp ground cumin

½ tsp ground turmeric

½ tsp dried chilli flakes

2 tbsp mild curry paste (ensure vegan)

2 rounded tbsp mango chutney

1 x 400ml (14fl oz) can of full-fat coconut milk

2 x 400g (14oz) cans of chickpeas (garbanzo beans), thoroughly drained and rinsed

2 tbsp coconut yogurt

generous pinch of sea salt

handful of coriander (cilantro) leaves, finely chopped

1 Heat the oil in a large pan, add the onion and garlic and cook over a medium-high heat for 2 minutes, then stir in the cumin, turmeric, chilli flakes, curry paste and mango chutney.

2 Pour in the coconut milk and chickpeas, then cook for 8 minutes, stirring frequently until the sauce is creamy.

3 Remove from the heat and lightly stir in the coconut yogurt. Season to taste with salt and scatter with coriander just before serving.

Speedy Tip

Freeze in portion-sized containers for an even speedier meal whenever you need it most. Simply defrost at room temperature, reheat thoroughly, and stir in some fresh coriander before serving.

CHEAT'S CHERRY AND CHOCOLATE GRANOLA CRUMBLE

SERVES 4

When you need a good dessert, but have no time to wait, cook up this comforting and satisfying crumble. Melted chocolate and hot cherries are a match made in heaven, especially when topped with crunchy granola, which saves you topping preparation time. I won't tell if you don't. Serve with a scoop of vegan vanilla ice cream.

450g (1lb) frozen cherries, defrosted

2 squares of dark chocolate (ensure dairy-free), grated, plus extra to serve

juice of ½ unwaxed lemon

2 tsp maple syrup

8 tbsp granola (ensure vegan)

1 Place the cherries, grated chocolate, lemon juice and maple syrup in a pan and cook over a medium-high heat for 4–5 minutes until bubbling. Stir frequently to avoid sticking and to ensure the chocolate is melting evenly.

2 Either spoon into individual bowls, or a larger serving dish, then sprinkle liberally with granola and extra grated chocolate just before serving.

Speedy Tip

If you don't have time to wait for the cherries to defrost, use the cherries frozen and cook for 10–12 minutes until piping hot.

GRILLED PINEAPPLE SUNDAES WITH RUM AND MACADAMIA NUTS

SERVES 4

This grown-up take on a sundae is sure to be a hit, not only because it fragrances the kitchen like a tropical island, but because each mouthful is pure decadence. I love to use vegan coconut ice cream in this dessert, but vegan vanilla works just as well.

6 tbsp dark spiced rum

4 tsp soft light brown sugar

pinch of ground cinnamon

1 small pineapple, peeled, cored and sliced into 8 rounds, or 8 slices of canned pineapple

2 tbsp macadamia nuts

4 scoops of dairy-free ice cream, preferably coconut flavour

2 tbsp toasted flaked coconut

a few small mint leaves, to garnish

1 In a large bowl, whisk together the rum, brown sugar and cinnamon. Dip the pineapple rings in the mix and set aside on a plate.

2 Heat a dry, large griddle (grill) pan over a high heat and use tongs to place the soaked pineapple rings into the pan. Cook for 2–3 minutes until hot and griddle marks appear, then use tongs to carefully turn the rings over to cook for a further 2 minutes.

3 Add any unused rum mix to the pan and cook for 1 minute, along with the macadamia nuts.

4 Place two pineapple rings per person on a serving plate, and place a scoop of ice cream on top. Scatter with flaked coconut, then drizzle over the hot rum mix and macadamias. Garnish with mint leaves and serve immediately.

Speedy Tip

The pineapple can be prepared and sliced a day in advance; simply refrigerate the pineapple in a little of its natural juice and bring to room temperature before soaking in the rum mix.

CHOCOLATE HAZELNUT POTS

SERVES 2

This is a 2-in-1 recipe that can be enjoyed warm (the melted chocolate will give a natural heat), or chill overnight for a more set dessert, depending on your mood or the season. Use hazelnut extract sparingly, as it has a concentrated flavour, but opt for the best quality you can afford.

340g (12oz) silken tofu, at room temperature

100g (3½oz) dark chocolate (ensure dairy-free)

4 tbsp maple syrup

1 tsp good-quality hazelnut extract

2 tbsp chopped hazelnuts

1 Add the silken tofu to a high-powered blender and blitz on high until smooth, or use a stick blender to blitz the silken tofu in a bowl.

2 Add the dark chocolate pieces to a heatproof bowl, then set over a pan of boiling water, ensuring the base of the bowl does not touch the water. Stir occasionally until the chocolate has melted into a shiny liquid, then carefully pour into the blended tofu.

3 Stir in the maple syrup and hazelnut extract, then blend again to combine fully.

4 Spoon into ramekin dishes and scatter with chopped hazelnuts before enjoying, or chill in the fridge for at least 4 hours.

Speedy Tip

Silken tofu gives a light and bubbly texture to this dessert, so save the extra-firm tofu for savoury recipes. You'll find silken tofu in supermarkets, usually in the ambient aisles.

TWO-MINUTE MUG CARROT CAKE

SERVES 1

When you need a cake fix quickly, you need this 2-minute cake made in the microwave, as a perfect portion for one. Feel free to throw in a few chopped pecans or walnuts, if you like.

4 tbsp self-raising flour

2 tbsp granulated sugar

pinch of ground cinnamon

pinch of grated nutmeg

½ carrot, peeled and finely grated

1 tsp golden raisins

4 tbsp sweetened soya milk

1 tbsp sunflower oil

1 tsp vanilla extract

1 rounded tbsp vegan cream cheese

2 tsp icing (confectioners') sugar

1 Mix together the flour, sugar, cinnamon and nutmeg in a large, microwave-proof mug.

2 Stir in the grated carrot and sultanas until coated in the flour mix.

3 Spoon in the soya milk, oil and vanilla extract and mix to create a thick batter, ensuring any dry mixture at the bottom gets combined.

4 Place the mug in a microwave and cook on high for 1 minute 30 seconds.

5 While the cake is cooking in the microwave, spoon the cream cheese into a bowl and mix in 1 teaspoon of the icing sugar. When this is combined, stir in the second teaspoon of icing sugar and mix again.

6 Carefully remove the mug from the microwave and allow to stand for 1 minute. Load on the cream cheese frosting and enjoy.

Speedy Tip

The ingredients are measured in spoon sizes, to save you from dusting off the scales!

STRAWBERRY AND BASIL CHEESECAKE PARFAIT

SERVES 4

Combine two pudding favourites – cheesecake and parfait – in this creamy and fruity dessert, with a hint of vibrant basil. Many brands of digestive biscuits are accidentally vegan, particularly supermarket own brands, but always check the label before you buy.

8 strawberries, roughly sliced

squeeze of lemon juice from an unwaxed lemon

6 basil leaves, torn

150g (5oz) vegan cream cheese

4 rounded tbsp strawberry soya yogurt

4 vegan digestive biscuits (graham crackers)

1 Add the sliced strawberries to a bowl and squeeze over the lemon juice. Stir in the basil leaves and leave to infuse while you complete the other steps.

2 In a bowl, whisk together the cream cheese and strawberry yogurt until combined. Set aside.

3 Place the digestive biscuits in a food-safe bag and beat with a rolling pin to create a fine crumb.

4 Layer the biscuit crumb, yogurt cream cheese and basil strawberries in glass ramekins or small glasses. Be generous, particularly with the cream cheese. Serve immediately.

Speedy Tip

Assemble just before serving to ensure the biscuit crumb stays crisp and crumbly.

20

MINUTES

EASY GRANOLA

MAKES ABOUT 10 PORTIONS

It's good to have a basic granola recipe that makes a few portions to last throughout the week. This combination of pumpkin seeds, pecans, cranberries and cinnamon is my favourite, but substitute for your preferred combinations such as hazelnut, dark chocolate chips and nutmeg. Store in a clean, sealed jar in a cool place for up to 2 weeks.

500g (5 cups) rolled oats

pinch of ground cinnamon

pinch of sea salt

4 tbsp pumpkin seeds

4 tbsp pecans, roughly chopped

200ml (generous ¾ cup) maple syrup

150ml (generous ½ cup) sunflower oil

4 tbsp dried cranberries

1 Preheat the oven to 180°C/350°F/gas mark 4.

2 In a large bowl, stir together the oats, cinnamon, sea salt, pumpkin seeds and pecans.

3 In a jug, lightly whisk together the maple syrup and sunflower oil. Pour this over the oat mixture and stir to combine.

4 Press firmly into a deep, non-stick baking tray (or two if they are of a smaller size), then bake in the oven for 15 minutes until golden.

5 Remove from the oven and allow to cool for a few minutes. Fork through the cooked oats to form clumps, then scatter through the cranberries. Allow to cool completely before transferring to a jar.

Speedy Tip

Use rolled oats rather than quick-cook oats for even cooking and a better crunch.

BREAKFAST BLISS BITES

SERVES 2 · SUITABLE FOR FREEZING

If you need to have breakfast on the go, these bite-sized treats are packed with energy-rich peanut butter, dark chocolate, seeds and oats to keep you going until lunch. Store in a cool place, in a sealed container, for up to 3 days.

2 rounded tbsp smooth peanut butter

6 tbsp rolled oats

1 tbsp dark chocolate chips (ensure dairy-free)

1 tbsp sesame seeds

pinch of sea salt

1 Spoon the peanut butter into a bowl along with 2 teaspoons of hot water.

2 Add the oats, chocolate chips, sesame seeds and salt and stir to combine into a stiff mixture.

3 Take tablespoon-sized amounts of the mixture and roll in your palms to form evenly sized balls. Place on a plate and chill in the fridge for at least 15 minutes until set.

Speedy Tip

The oil content of peanut butter varies from brand to brand, which means that you may need to add fewer or more oats. The mixture should be stiff enough to handle and roll.

ROASTED TOMATOES ON TOAST WITH SALSA VERDE

SERVES 2

Sweet, blistered roasted tomatoes served on thick, hot toast is a classic; here it's taken to the next level with salsa verde, which is packed with fresh herbs, pickles and extra virgin olive oil. This is my favourite lunch, which works equally as well for brunch or for a light supper.

300g (10oz) mixed baby tomatoes

drizzle of sunflower oil

30g (1oz) flat-leaf parsley

30g (1oz) basil leaves

generous drizzle of extra virgin olive oil

juice of ½ unwaxed lemon

2 pickled gherkins, diced

1 tbsp capers

generous pinch of sea salt

2 thick slices of sourdough bread

generous pinch of black pepper

1 Preheat the oven to 200°C/400°F/gas mark 6.

2 Place the tomatoes on a baking tray and drizzle with sunflower oil. Roast in the oven for 15–18 minutes until blistered and hot.

3 Meanwhile, prepare the salsa verde. Place the parsley and basil in a food processor or blender, drizzle in the olive oil and lemon juice and blitz until roughly combined. Alternatively, finely chop the fresh herbs then use a pestle and mortar to grind in the oil and lemon juice. Stir in the gherkins and capers and season with salt to taste.

4 Toast or grill the sliced sourdough until golden, then place on serving plates.

5 Remove the roasted tomatoes from the oven and season with pepper. Place on top of the toast and drizzle liberally with salsa verde.

Speedy Tip

You'll have some salsa verde left over – it will keep for up to 3 days in a sealed container in the fridge. Perfect for drizzling over pasta, brightening up soups, and adding extra flavour to falafel tagine (page 123).

CHICKPEA SCRAMBLE

SERVES 2 GENEROUSLY

This 20-minute breakfast uses pantry staples, along with some basic fresh ingredients, to create a filling and hearty start to the day. Serve as part of a full vegan breakfast, or on toast with sliced avocado.

1 x 400g (14oz) can of chickpeas (garbanzo beans), drained and rinsed

1 tbsp sunflower oil

6 button mushrooms, halved

6 cherry tomatoes, halved

generous handful of spinach leaves

2 spring onions (scallions), finely chopped

¼ tsp dried oregano

¼ tsp ground turmeric

pinch of sea salt and black pepper

1 Tip the chickpeas into a heatproof bowl and add in enough hot water to cover them. Allow to stand for 10 minutes, then drain away the water. Use a potato masher, or the back of a fork, to crush the chickpeas roughly, or blitz in a food processor.

2 In a large pan, heat the oil over a medium heat, then add the mushrooms and cook for 3–4 minutes until fragrant and softened. Add the cherry tomatoes, spinach, spring onions, oregano and turmeric and cook for a further 2 minutes.

3 Spoon the crushed chickpeas into the pan, and add 1 tablespoon of water. Stir to combine, then cook for 2 minutes until the chickpeas are hot and golden from the turmeric. Season to taste with salt and pepper.

Speedy Tip

I use canned chickpeas in this recipe as they are easy to source, but if you have any jarred chickpeas, you'll find they have a moreish flavour and a texture that is perfectly ready to scramble or mash. They are a little pricier, but will reduce the overall cooking time of the recipe.

HASH BROWN SHARER

SERVES 4 · SUITABLE FOR FREEZING

For me, hash browns are an essential part of a full vegan breakfast. Nothing beats that soft, golden bite! This is a larger, sharing version that is easy and quick to cook. The trick is to remove as much moisture as possible from the potatoes, and press the grated potatoes together firmly for the best texture all the way through. Grate the potatoes manually, or use the grater blade on a food processor.

3 large baking potatoes, grated (see Speedy Tip)

2 spring onions (scallions), finely chopped

generous pinch of sea salt and black pepper

4 tbsp sunflower oil

1   Lay the grated potatoes onto a clean tea towel. Squeeze out as much liquid as possible by twisting the tea towel over a sink. When the moisture has been removed, sprinkle in the spring onions and season with plenty of salt and pepper.

2   Heat the sunflower oil in a frying pan over a medium heat.

3   Combine the potato mixture into a dense, flat, round hash brown and place on a spatula. Slide into the hot pan and gently press the mixture down. Cook for 5–6 minutes until crisp and golden, then flip using the spatula and cook the other side for 5–6 minutes.

4   Slice into quarters and serve hot.

Speedy Tip

There's no need to peel the potatoes before grating, simply scrub clean and pat dry, for extra flavour and a rustic look.

BAKED BEAN BREAKFAST QUESADILLAS

SERVES 4

Turn a humble can of baked beans into something filling, fun and hearty for breakfast. I use plain tortilla wraps, but feel free to use seeded or herby versions if you prefer. Vegan 'cheddar style' hard cheese works well for these quesadillas; grate it finely to ensure it melts evenly throughout.

1 x 400g (14oz) can of baked beans in tomato sauce

1 tbsp barbecue sauce (ensure vegan)

pinch of sea salt and black pepper

small handful of spinach leaves, roughly shredded

2 spring onions (scallions), finely sliced

small handful of coriander (cilantro), finely chopped

50g (1¾oz) vegan hard cheese, finely grated

4 soft tortilla wraps

2 tbsp sunflower oil

1   Tip the baked beans into a bowl and roughly mash about half of them down with a fork. Stir in the barbecue sauce, salt and pepper.

2   Stir in the spinach leaves, spring onions, coriander and grated cheese until coated in the mix.

3   Lay out two tortilla wraps on a flat surface. Spoon the filling between each tortilla, then top with the remaining two tortillas.

4   Heat 1 tablespoon of the oil in a large frying pan and add a quesadillas. Cook for 3–4 minutes on each side until golden brown. Remove from the pan, then add the extra oil and cook the remaining quesadilla for 3–4 minutes on each side. Slice into quarters and serve.

Speedy Tip

Make up the filling the evening before and keep in the fridge until ready to use, for an even speedier breakfast.

TUSCAN BEANS WITH SAGE

SERVES 2 GENEROUSLY · SUITABLE FOR FREEZING

Tuscany loves to shine the spotlight on beans, with so many recipes using them as a staple protein. This Italian twist on canned baked beans uses sage and onion, with a pinch of chilli flakes for a little heat. Serve simply on toast, or over a jacket potato.

I tbsp sunflower oil

I onion, diced

2 garlic cloves, crushed

small handful sage leaves, finely chopped, plus extra to serve (or use I tsp dried sage)

pinch of dried chilli flakes

500g (2 cups/I7oz) passata (sieved tomatoes)

pinch of sugar

I x 400g (I4oz) can of cannellini beans, drained and rinsed

generous pinch of sea salt and black pepper

1   Heat the oil in a large pan, add the onion and soften over a medium heat for 2–3 minutes. Add the garlic, sage and chilli flakes and cook for a further 2 minutes.

2   Add the passata, sugar and cannellini beans and simmer for I5 minutes, stirring frequently.

3   Remove from the heat and season to taste with salt and plenty of pepper before topping with a few whole sage leaves to serve.

Speedy Tip

A pinch of sugar reduces the acidity of passata – either granulated or caster (superfine) sugar will work fine.

PINEAPPLE AND BLACK BEAN TOSTADAS

SERVES 2

Transform soft tortilla wraps by baking them in the oven until crisp and golden. This creates a tasty base for crushed avocado, spicy pineapple and black beans, alongside any condiments you fancy, including tomato salsa, vegan sour cream, or a few sprinkles of Tabasco.

2 large soft tortilla wraps

2 tsp sunflower oil

½ pineapple, flesh finely diced

1 x 400g (14oz) can of black beans, drained and rinsed

2 spring onions (scallions), finely sliced

2 radishes, thinly sliced

2 tsp sesame seeds

squeeze of juice from an unwaxed lime

generous pinches of smoked sea salt

1 avocado, peeled and halved

tortilla chips, to serve (optional)

hot sauce, to serve (ensure vegan) (optional)

1 Preheat the oven to 180°C/350°F/gas mark 4.

2 Arrange the tortilla wraps over two baking trays and brush with the sunflower oil. Bake in the oven for 8–10 minutes until golden brown and crisp.

3 In a bowl, stir together the pineapple, black beans, spring onions, radishes and sesame seeds. Squeeze over the lime juice and stir to distribute. Season to taste with smoked sea salt and allow to stand for a few minutes to infuse.

4 In a small bowl, crush the avocado using a fork until semi-smooth. Season with a little smoked sea salt.

5 Carefully remove the crisp tortillas from the oven and arrange on serving plates. Spoon on the avocado and smooth over the tortillas, taking care not to break them. Liberally load over the pineapple and black bean mix and serve with tortilla chips and hot sauce on the side, if you like.

Speedy Tip

The pineapple and black bean topping can be made up to 3 days in advance when kept in the fridge. It also makes a protein-packed side salad for a chilli, or even to load into a baked sweet potato.

CARAMELIZED ONION AND THYME PINWHEELS

MAKES 10

These versatile savoury pastries are perfect for packing in lunchboxes, sharing at a picnic, or even serving as an appetizer before a meal. Sometimes I add extra ingredients to the filling, including sundried tomatoes, grated vegan cheese or spinach, but the simplicity of sweet caramelized onions and thyme will always be my favourite. Although many brands of shop-bought puff pastry are vegan-friendly due to the use of vegetable oil instead of dairy butter, always check the ingredients before you buy.

1 tbsp sunflower oil

2 onions, thinly sliced

1 tsp soft light brown sugar

1 sprig of fresh thyme, leaves stripped from the stalk

generous pinch of sea salt and black pepper

1 sheet of shop-bought puff pastry (ensure vegan)

1 Add the oil and sliced onions to a large pan and cook over a medium heat for 5 minutes, stirring frequently.

2 Stir in the sugar and thyme leaves and turn up the heat to high to caramelize. Cook for a further 3 minutes until golden brown and fragrant. Season with salt and plenty of pepper.

3 Preheat the oven to 200°C/400°F/gas mark 6 and line a large baking tray with baking parchment.

4 Unroll the pastry sheet on a clean surface. Spoon the caramelized onions onto the pastry, then spread them out evenly right to the edges of the pastry.

5 Roll the pastry sheet up from top to bottom so you have one long 'log'. Use a sharp knife to cut the log into pinwheels, each one about 1cm (½in) wide to make about 10.

6 Place the pinwheels on the lined baking tray, then bake in the oven for 10 minutes until golden and cooked through. Serve warm or cold.

Speedy Tip

Remove the puff pastry sheet from the fridge 20 minutes before using to bring it to room temperature. The fats will warm up, so you will be able to roll the pastry without the risk of it cracking or leaking during cooking.

MUFFIN-TIN PIZZA PIES

MAKES 8

These bite-sized pizzas use tortilla wraps for crispy, baked edges – the perfect cheat's way to make a mini deep dish pizza. These are the perfect size for lunchboxes – for both adults and children! Feel free to add in other quick-cook toppings, such as pineapple, thinly sliced pepper and sundried tomatoes.

2 tsp sunflower oil

3 large tortilla wraps

3 tbsp tomato purée (paste)

150g (5oz) vegan hard cheese, grated

1 tbsp frozen or canned sweetcorn

pinch of dried oregano

4 button mushrooms, halved

4 cherry tomatoes, halved

8 small basil leaves

pinch of black pepper

1   Preheat the oven to 180°C/350°F/gas mark 4. Use a pastry brush to grease the cups of an 8-hole deep muffin tin with sunflower oil, then set aside.

2   Lay out the tortilla wraps on a flat surface. Use a cookie cutter (large enough to fill the muffin tin cup) to press out 16 circles.

3   Press one single tortilla round into each muffin cup, then brush the surface with a little oil. Press on another tortilla round to make a double layer.

4   In a bowl, stir together the tomato purée, grated cheese, sweetcorn and oregano, then spoon the mix evenly into the tortilla cups.

5   Press the mushrooms and tomatoes onto the mix, then bake in the oven for 10–12 minutes until the edges are golden and the filling is bubbling.

6   Carefully remove from the oven and allow to cool for a couple of minutes. Use a teaspoon to lift the pizzas from the tray and onto a serving plate. Top with the basil leaves and sprinkle with black pepper.

Speedy Tip

Cut out the tortilla bases and freeze in containers, to save you valuable preparation time when you make them again. The tortilla bases will defrost at room temperature in minutes.

PISTACHIO HERB SALAD

SERVES 2

A bowlful of this bright and fragrant salad will refresh your lunch break, with vibrant herbs, lemon juice and crunchy pistachios. It's easy to double the recipe for batch preparation, and the salad will keep for up to 4 days in the fridge.

150g (¾ cup) bulgar wheat

30g (1oz) flat-leaf parsley, finely chopped (including stalks)

30g (1oz) mint, leaves finely chopped

handful of dill, finely chopped

6 mixed baby tomatoes, roughly quartered

4 tbsp shelled pistachios

juice of 1 unwaxed lemon

drizzle of good-quality extra virgin olive oil

generous pinch of sea salt

1　Add the bulgar wheat to a heatproof bowl and pour over enough boiling water to just cover it. Place a plate over the bowl or cover tightly with cling film (plastic wrap) and allow to stand for 15 minutes.

2　Fork through the bulgar wheat and transfer to a larger bowl. Stir in the parsley, mint and dill until evenly distributed, then stir in the tomatoes and pistachios.

3　Squeeze in the lemon juice and stir in the olive oil until combined. Season to taste with salt.

Speedy Tip

Store lemons in the fridge for freshness, but bring to room temperature before squeezing to release more juice.

BRUSCHETTA

SERVES 4

Dream of blue seas, clear skies and long lunches with this Greek-inspired bruschetta. It's the perfect summertime lunch, or addition to your evening aperitivo. Crumble over some vegan feta, if you like.

I yellow (bell) pepper, finely diced

I red (bell) pepper, diced

6 cherry tomatoes, roughly quartered

½ small red onion, finely sliced

4cm (I½in) piece of cucumber, sliced

I2 pitted black olives

small handful of flat-leaf parsley, finely chopped

generous drizzle of extra virgin olive oil

pinch of sea salt and black pepper

I white baguette (French stick), cut into 2.5cm (Iin) slices

I In a bowl, stir together both peppers, the tomatoes, onion, cucumber, olives and parsley. Toss through the olive oil and season with salt and plenty of pepper.

2 Grill or toast the slices of bread until lightly golden, then top with spoonfuls of the salad.

Speedy Tip

The salad topping can be made up to 2 days in advance when kept in the fridge, and is also delicious loaded into flatbreads and served with houmous.

SAVOURY, SMOKY YOGURT BOWLS

SERVES 2

Swirl cool lime and smoked, salted yogurt into bowls and top with paprika-roasted sweet potatoes, peppers and red onion, with a hint of chilli. Who said yogurt is just for breakfast or dessert? Perfect for a satisfying lunch, or as a light evening meal.

I large sweet potato, peeled and cut into Icm (½in) cubes

I red (bell) pepper, finely sliced

I red onion, thinly sliced

2 tbsp sunflower oil

½ tsp smoked paprika

pinch of dried chilli flakes

500g (17oz) soya yogurt, chilled

zest and I tbsp juice of I unwaxed lime

generous pinch of smoked sea salt

pinch of black pepper

2 tbsp toasted pine nuts

small handful of coriander (cilantro), roughly torn

1   Preheat the oven to 200°C/400°F/gas mark 6.

2   Add the diced sweet potato, red pepper and onion to a bowl and stir in the sunflower oil, smoked paprika and chilli flakes. Stir to coat the vegetables.

3   Spoon the vegetables into a roasting tin, then roast in the oven for 15–18 minutes until the sweet potato has softened.

4   Meanwhile in another bowl, stir together the soya yogurt, lime zest and juice until combined. Season to taste with smoked sea salt and black pepper. Spoon into serving bowls.

5   Remove the tin from the oven and spoon the roasted vegetables over the yogurt. Season with sea salt and scatter with pine nuts and coriander.

Speedy Tip

Dicing the sweet potato to Icm (½in) cubes ensures it will roast in a speedy 15–18 minutes. Larger pieces will result in a longer cooking time.

CREAMY MUSHROOM SOUP

SERVES 4 · SUITABLE FOR FREEZING

Simple, hearty comfort food that fuels lunches throughout autumn and winter. Chestnut mushrooms give the best, earthy flavour here, and a warmer colour too. If you don't have a high-powered jug blender, a stick blender will work fine, although it may take a little while longer to blitz until smooth. Delicious served with seeded crackers.

I tbsp sunflower oil

I onion, chopped

500g (1lb 2oz) chestnut mushrooms, brushed clean and sliced

I garlic clove, crushed

400ml (generous 1½ cups) hot vegetable stock

100ml (scant ½ cup) single (light) soya cream, plus extra (optional) to serve

generous pinch of sea salt and black pepper

small handful of flat-leaf parsley, chopped

1 Heat the oil in a large pan, add the onion and cook over a medium-high heat for 2–3 minutes until softened. Add the mushrooms and cook for 5–6 minutes, stirring frequently to avoid sticking, then add the garlic and cook for a further minute. Remove a spoonful of mushrooms and reserve for garnishing.

2 Pour in the hot vegetable stock and cook at a gentle simmer for a further 5 minutes. Remove from the heat and allow to stand for a couple of minutes before stirring in the soya cream.

3 Pour into a high-powered blender jug and blitz until completely smooth. Season to taste with salt and pepper.

4 Pour or ladle into warmed bowls and spoon over the reserved mushrooms. Scatter over the chopped parsley and finish with a little extra black pepper and a drizzle of cream, if you like.

Speedy Tip

Soya, oat or pea-based dairy-free pouring creams all work well in this recipe. If you don't have any dairy-free cream available, use an unsweetened plant-based milk. It will have a less creamy mouthfeel, so reduce the amount of stock used by 3 tablespoons to compensate.

GRILLED AUBERGINE SALAD

SERVES 2

This full-of-flavour salad has warm, grilled aubergine, pan-roasted red onions, pops of juicy pomegranate and a creamy harissa dressing. Perfect for al fresco lunches, when the griddle pan can be switched for the barbecue.

2 tbsp sunflower oil

I aubergine (eggplant), thinly sliced lengthways

I red onion, quartered

2 generous handfuls of wild rocket (arugula)

generous handful of flat-leaf parsley leaves, roughly torn

4 cherry tomatoes, halved

juice of ¼ unwaxed lemon

2 rounded tbsp soya yogurt

½ tsp harissa paste

generous pinch of sea salt

seeds of I pomegranate

1   Heat the oil in a large griddle (grill) pan over a medium-high heat, then use tongs to add the aubergine strips and red onion quarters. Depending on the size of the pan, you may have to do this in batches. Turn the aubergine and onion after 2–3 minutes, or when grill lines appear and the aubergine becomes soft.

2   Meanwhile, in a large bowl, toss together the rocket, parsley and tomatoes. Drizzle through the lemon juice and distribute between serving plates or onto a serving platter.

3   In a smaller bowl, gently stir together the soya yogurt and harissa, then season with sea salt.

4   Place the griddled aubergine and onion over the salad leaves, then drizzle over the harissa yogurt. Scatter over the pomegranate seeds.

Speedy Tip

To save time (and reduce mess!) prepared pomegranate seeds are available from most supermarkets.

HERBY SPRING SOUP WITH FREGOLA

SERVES 4 · SUITABLE FOR FREEZING

Cooler spring days call for a bowl of soup, packed with seasonal vegetables and herbs. Fregola is a small, round pasta that sits perfectly on a soup spoon, and makes the bowlful more filling and satisfying for lunch or a light supper. You'll find dried fregola in most supermarkets, but do read the ingredients to make sure it is egg-free.

I tbsp sunflower oil

I leek, thinly sliced

I garlic clove, crushed

I courgette (zucchini), sliced

150g (5oz) fine green beans, trimmed and roughly chopped

I x 400g (14oz) can of haricot beans, drained and rinsed

I litre (4 cups) hot vegetable stock

3 tbsp dried fregola (ensure egg-free)

30g (1oz) basil, finely chopped

generous handful of flat-leaf parsley, finely chopped

generous pinch of sea salt and black pepper

1 Heat the sunflower oil in a large pan, add the leek and cook over a medium-high heat for 2–3 minutes, then add the garlic, courgette and green beans and cook for a further 2 minutes.

2 Add the haricot beans, vegetable stock and fregola and bring to the boil, then simmer for 12 minutes until the vegetables are tender and the pasta has softened.

3 Remove from the heat and stir through the chopped basil and parsley. Season to taste with salt and pepper.

Speedy Tip

Finely chop the fresh basil and flat-leaf parsley stalks as well as the leaves, as they are also packed with flavour. A handful of fresh mint or dill makes a lovely addition too.

BRAISED CHICKPEAS WITH CHILLI, ORANGE AND TOMATO

SERVES 2 GENEROUSLY · SUITABLE FOR FREEZING

Canned chickpeas are a store cupboard staple – so let's make them the star of the show in this simple supper. Braising the chickpeas in oil with garlic and chilli flakes infuses them before simmering in tomatoes and finishing with freshly squeezed orange juice. If you can't source a savoy cabbage, chop up a few leaves of cavolo nero. Serve with some warm bread, or buttery mashed potatoes.

I tbsp sunflower oil

I onion, diced

¼ tsp dried chilli flakes

3 garlic cloves, crushed

½ savoy cabbage, leaves roughly sliced

I x 400g (I4oz) can of chickpeas (garbanzo beans), drained and rinsed

I x 400g (I4oz) can of cherry tomatoes

I tbsp tomato purée (paste)

pinch of sugar

zest and juice of I unwaxed orange

generous pinch of sea salt

handful of flat-leaf parsley, finely chopped

1 Heat the oil a large pan, add the onion and chilli flakes and cook over a medium-high heat for 2 minutes until the onion has softened. Add the garlic, cabbage and chickpeas and cook for 3 minutes, stirring constantly to infuse the chickpeas with the flavours.

2 Stir in the canned cherry tomatoes, tomato purée and pinch of sugar. Bring to a simmer then reduce to a medium heat and loosely place a lid over the pan. Cook for 10–12 minutes, stirring occasionally.

3 Remove the pan from the heat and stir in the orange zest and juice. Season to taste with sea salt, then scatter with flat-leaf parsley just before serving.

Speedy Tip

You can find canned cherry tomatoes in most supermarkets. They have a sweeter taste than standard canned chopped tomatoes, which works perfectly with the zesty orange flavour.

TAMARIND, MUSHROOM AND BROCCOLI SKEWERS

SERVES 2

Grilled mushrooms take on an intense, deep flavour when marinated in tamarind and sweet, smoky maple syrup. Allow Tenderstem broccoli to gently char on the grilling skewers, then freshen up the dish with pops of parsley and spring onions. Serve with warmed flatbreads, toasted pittas, or with pistachio herb salad (page 100).

2 tbsp olive oil, plus extra for brushing the pan

2 tbsp maple syrup

1 tbsp tamarind paste

½ tsp ground cinnamon

pinch of dried chilli flakes

12 chestnut mushrooms, brushed clean

12 stems of Tenderstem broccoli

2 spring onions (scallions), finely sliced

small handful of flat-leaf parsley, finely chopped

pinch of sea salt

1 In a large bowl, whisk together the olive oil, maple syrup, tamarind paste, cinnamon and chilli flakes.

2 Stir in the mushrooms and coat in the tamarind mix.

3 Shake off the excess mix, then thread a mushroom onto a metal skewer (or a pre-soaked wooden skewer) followed by a piece of Tenderstem broccoli. Repeat until the skewers are filled.

4 Brush a griddle (grill) pan with a little olive oil and place over a high heat. Once the griddle pan is hot, lay on the skewers and cook for 8–10 minutes, turning frequently for even cooking.

5 Remove the skewers from the pan and place on plates. Scatter with spring onions, parsley and sea salt, then serve.

Speedy Tip

You can find jars of tamarind paste in most large supermarkets. It is a versatile ingredient, perfect for adding a deep, tangy and slightly sour flavour to tagines, sauces and barbecue marinades. Simply stir in a spoonful for extra flavour, and store the jar in the fridge.

PB&J TOFU

SERVES 2 GENEROUSLY

Sweet chilli jam and a spicy peanut (butter) sauce take tofu from plain to incredible, in just a few easy steps. The tofu becomes golden and sticky, with lashings of smooth and gently spiced peanut sauce lifting the dish to the next level. To save time, buy pre-pressed extra-firm tofu. Serve with steamed rice, or noodles and vegetables.

I tbsp sunflower oil

280g (10oz) extra-firm tofu, drained and blotted, sliced into triangles

4 tbsp chilli jam (ensure vegan)

2 rounded tbsp smooth peanut butter

I tbsp dark soy sauce

pinch of dried chilli flakes

juice of ½ unwaxed lime

I spring onion (scallion), finely sliced

small handful of coriander (cilantro) leaves, roughly torn

1   Heat the oil in a large pan over a medium-high heat, then add the tofu triangles. Cook for 5–6 minutes on each side until light golden. Spoon in the chilli jam and coat the tofu until bubbling.

2   Meanwhile, add the peanut butter and soy sauce to another pan, along with 4 tablespoons of hot water. Use a balloon whisk to mix into a smooth paste, then add the chilli flakes and lime juice and whisk again.

3   Arrange the tofu on serving plates and drizzle over spoonfuls of the peanut sauce. Scatter over the spring onion and coriander leaves and serve hot.

Speedy Tip

If you don't have sweet chilli jam available, sweet chilli sauce is a great alternative, but read the ingredients to ensure that it does not contain fish.

SPICED BHAJI NAAN WRAPS

SERVES 2 GENEROUSLY

Pillowy naan breads are loaded with hot, spiced onion bhajis, minty yogurt and mango chutney. I like to throw in some shredded lettuce and coriander for crunch, too. It's worth making these onion bhajis from scratch, as they are full of flavour (and easier to make than you'd think). They're worthy of being the star of the show – instead of always the side dish!

5 tbsp plain (all-purpose) flour

I tsp cumin seeds

I tsp garam masala

pinch of dried chilli flakes

I tsp sea salt

2 onions, thinly sliced

500ml (2 cups) sunflower oil, for frying

2 rounded tbsp thick coconut yogurt

small handful of mint leaves, finely chopped

2 naan breads (ensure vegan)

handful of lettuce, shredded

¼ cucumber, thinly sliced lengthways

small handful of coriander (cilantro) leaves, roughly torn

4 tsp mango chutney

1   In a bowl, stir together the flour, cumin seeds, garam masala, chilli flakes and salt. Stir in the sliced onion and coat in the dry mixture. Stir in 3 tablespoons of cold water to create a thick, even mixture.

2   Heat the sunflower oil in a large, heavy-based pan over a medium-high heat. Test if the oil is hot enough by dripping a small amount of the bhaji batter into the pan – it should sizzle, rise to the surface and become golden. Carefully spoon tablespoon-sized amounts of the mixture into the hot oil, working in batches of 3–4 bhajis at a time to avoid overcrowding and sticking. Cook for 4–5 minutes until golden. Drain on kitchen paper and keep warm while you cook the rest of the bhajis.

3   In a small bowl, stir together the coconut yogurt and mint leaves, then set aside.

4   Warm the naan breads in an oven preheated to 160°C/320°F/gas mark 3 for 3–4 minutes. Remove and place on serving plates.

5   Add shredded lettuce, cucumber and coriander to each naan and top with a spoonful of the minty yogurt. Lay in the onion bhajis, then spoon over the mango chutney. Wrap, and enjoy hot.

Speedy Tip

Some brands of shop-bought naan bread contain cow's milk, but vegan-friendly brands are available in large supermarkets. Before warming the naan breads, drip over some water to avoid them drying out. Look out for garlic and coriander flavoured varieties to add extra flavour.

COURGETTE PESTO

SERVES 2 GENEROUSLY

This lighter version of a classic pesto uses roasted courgettes, which provide flavour and moisture without needing to add lots of oil to the mix. Stir through your favourite pasta, drizzle over pizza, mash into potatoes or use as a dip for toasted pitta breads.

2 medium courgettes (zucchini), roughly chopped into half-rounds

1 tbsp sunflower oil

4 tbsp pine nuts

1 garlic clove, peeled

30g (1oz) fresh basil

juice of 1 unwaxed lemon

20g (¾oz) vegan hard cheese, finely grated

generous pinch of black pepper

1   Preheat the oven to 200°C/400°F/gas mark 6.

2   Arrange the courgettes on a baking tray and drizzle with the oil. Roast in the oven for 15 minutes.

3   Add the pine nuts to a dry frying pan and toast over a high heat for 2–3 minutes until golden brown and fragrant, then set aside.

4   Remove the roasted courgette from the oven and allow to cool for a few minutes. Meanwhile, add the garlic, basil and lemon juice to a food processor or blender and blitz roughly.

5   Add the courgette to the food processor or blender and blitz until roughly combined.

6   Stir in the grated cheese and season to taste with black pepper. Finish by scattering in the toasted pine nuts.

Speedy Tip

If you don't have pine nuts available, flaked almonds make a delicious alternative. Toast them in the same way you would with pine nuts – this toasting step is well worth it as it brings out the buttery flavour of the nuts.

FALAFEL TAGINE

SERVES 4 GENEROUSLY · SUITABLE FOR FREEZING

Store-bought falafel are given life in this recipe, as they sit like flavourful dumplings in the tagine, which is made on the stove top for speed. This is the perfect fuss-free midweek meal, using store cupboard ingredients to their full potential. Serve with pistachio herb salad (page 100) or some simple couscous.

2 tbsp sunflower oil

I red onion, roughly chopped

I carrot, peeled and roughly chopped

I aubergine (eggplant), evenly diced

handful of fine green beans, trimmed and roughly halved

I yellow (bell) pepper, roughly chopped

2 garlic cloves, crushed

2cm (¾in) piece of ginger, peeled and grated

2 tsp ras el hanout

500g (2 cups/17oz) passata (sieved tomatoes)

I tbsp maple syrup

2 tsp harissa paste

I x 400g (14oz) can of chickpeas (garbanzo beans), drained and rinsed

8 dried apricots

juice of I unwaxed lemon

generous pinch of sea salt

8 ready-to-eat falafel (ensure vegan)

handful of flat-leaf parsley, finely chopped

1   Heat the oil in a large pan, add the onion, carrot, aubergine, green beans and yellow pepper and cook over a medium-high heat for 4 minutes, stirring frequently, until the vegetables have begun to soften. Add the garlic, ginger and ras el hanout and cook for a further minute.

2   Pour in the passata and spoon in the maple syrup and harissa paste, then stir in the chickpeas and apricots and simmer for 12 minutes until the liquid has reduced a little.

3   Remove from the heat and through the lemon juice. Season to taste with salt.

4   Lay over the falafel and allow to warm through for a couple of minutes, before serving scattered with the parsley.

Speedy Tip

Ras el hanout is a Middle Eastern spice blend, with all the familiar flavours of tagine, including cumin, cinnamon, turmeric and cardamom. This all-in-one mix saves any blending time and can also be used to sprinkle on roasted vegetables, stirred through yogurt for a savoury twist, or rubbed over tofu before grilling.

SPRING ORZOTTO

SERVES 4

Fancy a fresh and seasonal risotto in just 20 minutes? This recipe uses orzo instead of rice, for a quick and easy risotto – which doesn't require constant stirring! Just like risotto made with arborio rice, some prefer the dish thicker, while some prefer a little more liquid, so add in most of the stock when cooking, and reserve a little to stir through later if it appears too thick.

I tbsp sunflower oil

I onion, diced

2 garlic cloves, crushed

pinch of dried chilli flakes

300g (10oz) dried orzo (ensure egg-free)

800ml (3⅓ cups) hot vegetable stock

200g (7oz) asparagus, chopped into lengths

50g (1¾oz) fine green beans, trimmed and chopped into lengths

generous handful of spring greens, thinly sliced

3 tbsp frozen peas

zest and juice of I unwaxed lemon

generous pinch of sea salt and black pepper

small handful of basil leaves

a few wild garlic flowers, to serve (optional)

1   Heat the oil in a large pan, add the onion and cook over a medium-high heat for 2–3 minutes until softened. Add the garlic and chilli flakes and cook for another minute.

2   Stir in the orzo and vegetable stock and bring to the boil, then add the asparagus, green beans and spring greens. Reduce the heat and cook at a gentle simmer for 12 minutes.

3   Stir in the frozen peas, lemon zest and juice and cook for a further minute.

4   Season to taste with salt and pepper before spooning into bowls. Scatter over the basil leaves and wild garlic flowers (optional) just before serving.

Speedy Tip

Orzo is rice-shaped pasta, and is a speedy alternative to rice in risotto, but is also versatile and can be used in soups, salads and stews. Most dried varieties do not contain egg, but always check the label before you buy.

AUBERGINE, MUSHROOM AND YOGURT STROGANOFF

SERVES 4

Yogurt creates a tangy and light sauce for this stroganoff, which is packed with umami mushrooms and meaty aubergine. I love the depth of flavour that smoked paprika brings to the dish, but if you only have sweet paprika to hand, that will work just fine. Serve with rice, ribboned pasta or my buttered root mash with nutmeg (overleaf).

2 tbsp sunflower oil

I large aubergine (eggplant), cut evenly into 3cm (1¼in) pieces

12 button mushrooms, brushed clean

I red onion, diced

3 garlic cloves, crushed

I rounded tsp smoked paprika

I tbsp soy sauce

500g (17oz) soya yogurt

squeeze of juice from an unwaxed lemon

pinch of sea salt and black pepper

handful of flat-leaf parsley

1   Heat I tablespoon of the oil in a large wok over a high heat, then add the aubergine and cook for 4–5 minutes, stirring frequently, until the aubergine starts to get some golden brown colour.

2   Reduce the heat to medium and add the remaining tablespoon of sunflower oil, the mushrooms and onion, then stir-fry for 2 minutes. Add the garlic and smoked paprika and cook for a further minute.

3   Stir in the soy sauce and soya yogurt, then reduce the heat to low-medium. Heat for 10 minutes, stirring frequently to combine.

4   Remove the wok from the heat and stir in the lemon juice. Season to taste with salt and pepper. Scatter with flat-leaf parsley just before serving.

Speedy Tip

Use a wok to quickly cook the aubergine and mushrooms; the high heat will add colour and flavour to the dish. Reduce the heat to low-medium when you stir in the yogurt, to avoid it sticking or separating.

BUTTERED ROOT MASH WITH NUTMEG

SERVES 4 · SUITABLE FOR FREEZING

If you're looking for a satisfying and speedy side to go with your favourite vegan sausages or pie, then look no further than this comforting mash. Switching potatoes for root vegetables gives you a quicker cooking time and autumnal flavours, and is a great way to sneak in the vegetables. Oat or soya pouring cream works well in this dish, or use an unsweetened plant-based milk of your choice, if you prefer. Delicious with aubergine, mushroom and yogurt stroganoff (page 127).

4 parsnips, peeled and roughly chopped

4 carrots, peeled and roughly chopped

1 swede (rutabaga), peeled and roughly chopped

½ small butternut squash, peeled and roughly chopped

2 rounded tbsp vegan butter

4 tbsp single (light) plant-based cream

small handful of chives, finely chopped

generous pinch of sea salt and black pepper

pinch of freshly grated nutmeg

1 Bring a large pan of water to the boil over a medium-high heat, then add in the parsnips, carrots, swede and butternut squash. Simmer for 15 minutes until softened.

2 Remove from the heat and drain away the water thoroughly. Spoon in the butter and cream, then use a potato masher to pound into a smooth and creamy mash.

3 Stir in the chives, salt and pepper, then finish with a little grated nutmeg. Serve hot.

Speedy Tip

Chop all of the vegetables roughly the same size for even cooking times: 2cm (¾in) pieces will cook through in 15 minutes, larger pieces may take longer.

Pictured on page 126.

PIZZA PASTA

SERVES 2 GENEROUSLY

With all of the flavours of your favourite pizza, this speedy supper is the perfect midweek alternative to calling for a pizza delivery. Feel free to throw over some shop-bought croutons for extra crunch, or make your own by roughly dicing a slice of day-old white bread, drizzling with olive oil and baking for 8–10 minutes at 200°C/400°F/gas mark 6.

I tbsp sunflower oil

½ small red onion, thinly sliced

I red (bell) pepper, thinly sliced

4 chestnut mushrooms, brushed clean and thinly sliced

handful of pitted black olives, sliced

I garlic clove, crushed

½ tsp dried oregano

500g (2 cups/17oz) passata (sieved tomatoes)

pinch of granulated sugar

150g (5oz) dried penne pasta (ensure egg-free)

30g (1oz) vegan hard cheese, grated

generous pinch of sea salt and black pepper

small handful of small basil leaves

1 Heat the oil a large pan over a medium heat, then add the onion, pepper, mushrooms and olives. Stir for 3–4 minutes until the vegetables begin to soften.

2 Stir in the garlic and oregano and cook for a further minute.

3 Pour in the passata and stir in the sugar. Loosely place a lid over the pan and reduce the heat to medium-low. Cook for 10 minutes, stirring occasionally.

4 Meanwhile, bring a separate pan of water to the boil over a medium-high heat, then add the pasta. Cook for 9–10 minutes until al dente; remove from the heat and then drain away the water.

5 Add the drained pasta to the sauce and stir to combine. Stir in the grated cheese and cook for a further minute to melt the cheese.

6 Remove from the heat and season to taste with salt and pepper. Spoon into serving bowls and scatter with basil leaves.

Speedy Tip

Penne pasta is my preferred choice, as I love the way the herby sauce sits in the tubes. Fusilli, rigatoni and macaroni make good alternatives.

EASIEST-EVER MEDITERRANEAN BAKE

SERVES 2

This easy traybake is perfect for weeknights, and is packed with lots of quick-cooked vegetables. Use shop-bought focaccia for the crispy croutons, but do check that it is vegan friendly. This recipe is easy to double up when cooking for a family.

I garlic clove, bruised

200g (7oz) cherry tomatoes

I red (bell) pepper, thickly sliced

I yellow (bell) pepper, thickly sliced

I red onion, peeled and cut into wedges

handful of fine green beans, trimmed

8 pitted black olives

2 tbsp blanched almonds

pinch of dried oregano

100g (3½oz) focaccia, roughly torn into 3cm (1¼in) chunks

generous glug of olive oil

juice of ¼ unwaxed lemon

generous pinch of sea salt and black pepper

handful of fresh basil leaves

1   Preheat the oven to 200°C/400°F/gas mark 6.

2   Rub the bruised garlic over the inside of a large, deep roasting tin, releasing the fragrant oils, then leave in the tin.

3   Add the cherry tomatoes, peppers, onion, green beans, olives and almonds to the roasting tin and stir to combine. Sprinkle over the oregano.

4   Scatter the chunks of focaccia over the top, then drizzle the whole lot with olive oil.

5   Bake in the oven for 15–18 minutes until the vegetables have softened and the focaccia is crisp at the edges.

6   Remove from the oven and squeeze over the lemon juice. Season with salt and pepper and scatter with basil leaves just before serving.

Speedy Tip
Rubbing the roasting tin with a bashed or bruised garlic clove give an extra layer of flavour and fragrance to the traybake.

MANGO AND COCONUT CURRY

SERVES 4 · SUITABLE FOR FREEZING

Mango is a versatile fruit, perfect for enjoying at breakfast, or chopping into a salad for lunch. It is also delicious and tender cooked into a creamy coconut curry, made with gentle spices, green beans and wilted spinach. If you're serving more people, or to increase the protein content of the dish, throw in a can of green lentils along with the coconut milk. Serve with fragrant basmati rice.

I tbsp sunflower oil

I onion, diced

½ tsp mustard seeds

generous pinch of dried chilli flakes

I tsp ground cumin

I tsp ground turmeric

2 garlic cloves, crushed

I rounded tbsp mild curry paste (ensure vegan)

2 x 400ml (14fl oz) cans of full-fat coconut milk

2 firm unpeeled mangoes, washed clean and sliced into wedges

100g (3½oz) fine green beans, trimmed and halved

I tbsp mango chutney

generous handful of spinach leaves

I tbsp flaked almonds

I tbsp desiccated (dried shredded) coconut

juice of I unwaxed lemon

generous pinch of sea salt

handful of coriander (cilantro) leaves, roughly torn

1   Heat the oil in a large pan, add the onion, mustard seeds and chilli flakes and cook over a medium-high heat for 2–3 minutes until the onion begins to soften and the mustard seeds begin to make popping sounds. Stir in the cumin, turmeric and garlic and cook for another minute.

2   Stir in the curry paste and pour in the coconut milk. Add in the mango wedges and green beans, then cook for 10 minutes, stirring occasionally.

3   Stir in the mango chutney and spinach leaves and cook for a further 5 minutes.

4   Meanwhile, toast the flaked almonds and desiccated coconut together in a separate dry frying pan for 2 minutes until golden and fragrant, then set aside.

5   Remove the mango curry from the heat and gently stir in the lemon juice and season to taste with salt. Sprinkle with the toasted almonds, desiccated coconut and coriander leaves just before serving.

Speedy Tip

There's no need to peel the mangoes for use in this curry. The skin is edible, and prevents the fruit becoming too soft during cooking.

RICE PUDDING WITH CHERRIES

SERVES 2 GENEROUSLY

Creamy, sweet rice pudding is topped with dark, cinnamon-scented cherries and a sprinkle of brown sugar in my favourite version of the classic dessert. This is pure comfort food for autumn and winter nights.

100g (generous ½ cup) flaked pudding rice

800ml (3⅓ cups) vanilla-flavoured soya milk

2 rounded tbsp caster (superfine) sugar

200g (7oz) fresh or frozen cherries, pitted

zest and juice of 1 unwaxed lemon

2 tbsp maple syrup

1 cinnamon stick

2 pinches of brown sugar

1 Tip the rice into a large pan and stir in the soya milk and caster sugar. Bring to a simmer over a low-medium heat and cook for 10–15 minutes, stirring frequently, until thickened.

2 Put the cherries, lemon zest and juice, maple syrup and the cinnamon stick into another pan and cook over a low-medium heat for 10–15 minutes, stirring frequently to avoid sticking, until shiny and bubbling.

3 Spoon the rice pudding into warmed bowls. Spoon the hot cherries over the rice pudding, then sprinkle with a pinch of brown sugar.

Speedy Tip

Vanilla-flavoured soya milk can be found in most supermarkets, but if you don't have this available, feel free to switch for a sweetened plant-based milk of your choice and add in 1 teaspoon of good-quality vanilla extract.

STRAWBERRY AND CREAM CHEESE PUFFS

SERVES 6

If you're looking for a quick and simple dessert to impress friends, look no further than this summery strawberry tart. Many brands of shop-bought puff pastry use vegetable fat instead of dairy butter, therefore making it suitable for vegans, but always check the label before you buy. Switch the strawberries for sliced kiwis, raspberries or mango, for endless variations throughout the summer.

1 sheet of ready-rolled puff pastry (ensure dairy-free)

2 tsp soya milk

4 rounded tbsp vegan cream cheese

½ tsp vanilla extract

200g (7oz) strawberries, thinly sliced

finely grated zest of 1 unwaxed lime

icing (confectioners') sugar, for dusting

1 Preheat the oven to 220°C/425°F/gas mark 7. Line a large baking tray with baking parchment.

2 Unroll the pastry onto the baking tray. Fold in the edges of the pastry by 2cm (¾in) to make a border crust, then brush the crust lightly with soya milk. Prick the centre of the pastry with a fork a few times, then bake in the oven for 10–12 minutes until golden.

3 Remove the pastry from the oven and use a fork to press the centre down, if it has risen. Allow to cool.

4 Meanwhile, use a balloon whisk to combine the cream cheese and vanilla extract in a bowl, until light and fluffy.

5 Spread the cream cheese mix generously over the centre of the cooled pastry. Top with the sliced strawberries.

6 Grate over the lime zest and dust with icing sugar just before serving.

Speedy Tip

Whip the vanilla cream cheese up to a day in advance and keep in the fridge, but take out of the fridge an hour before use to make it easier to spread onto the puff pastry base.

GRILLED PEACH MELBA WITH RASPBERRY SAUCE

SERVES 4

Give this retro pudding a revamp, by grilling the peaches in vegan cinnamon butter before drizzling with a zesty raspberry sauce. I love this hot dessert served with vegan vanilla ice cream, but it is also delicious served with a spoonful of thick coconut yogurt, or a drizzle of cool vegan pouring cream.

200g (7oz) raspberries

1 rounded tbsp icing (confectioners') sugar

zest of ½ unwaxed lemon

2 tsp vegan butter

pinch of ground cinnamon

4 large, ripe peaches, halved and stones removed, or use 4 canned peaches

4 scoops of vegan vanilla ice cream

1 Add the raspberries, icing sugar and lemon zest to a pan, place over a medium heat and bring to a simmer, crushing the raspberries from time to time. Cook for 10 minutes until bubbling, then allow to stand for a few minutes. At this stage you can strain the sauce through a sieve to remove the pips, if you like.

2 Heat the butter and cinnamon in a griddle (grill) pan over a low heat until melted. Turn up the heat to high then place the peach halves onto the grill, cut side down.

3 Grill for 5–6 minutes until softened and char lines appear. Turn the peaches and cook for a further 2 minutes.

4 Place the grilled peaches in serving bowls and drizzle generously with the raspberry sauce. Spoon on the ice cream just before serving.

Speedy Tip

The raspberry sauce can be made up to 2 days in advance when kept in the fridge. Simply reheat in a pan before serving.

CHOCOLATE AND BANANA TORTILLA POCKETS

SERVES 2

Everyone will love these sweet and hot tortilla pockets, filled with rich and gooey chocolate and banana. Think of them as a sweet quesadilla, with a buttery, toasted tortilla and a hot centre. A fun pudding or snack for any time of the day.

I tbsp vegan butter

pinch of ground cinnamon

2 large white tortilla wraps

2 tbsp chocolate spread (ensure vegan)

I banana, peeled and thinly sliced

pinch of demerara sugar

1 Melt the butter in a pan or a microwave for a few seconds until liquid. Stir in the cinnamon.

2 Brush one side of each tortilla with the melted butter mix, using a pastry brush.

3 Turn the tortilla so the buttered side is underneath. Smooth I tablespoon of chocolate spread on each tortilla, leaving a 2cm (¾in) border around the edge (as the chocolate spread will melt a little when cooking).

4 Place slices of the banana on top of the chocolate spread (on one half only), then fold the tortilla in half.

5 Heat a frying pan over a medium-high heat, then place one of the folded tortillas in the pan, cooking until golden for 3–4 minutes on each side. Repeat with the other tortilla wrap.

6 Remove from the pan and sprinkle the tops with a little sugar. Cut in half and serve hot.

Speedy Tip

Vegan chocolate spread can be found in many supermarkets, and in some good-quality chocolate shops too. For a delicious alternative, choose a caramelized biscuit spread, or peanut butter.

CHAI-SPICED SCONES

SERVES 6 · SUITABLE FOR FREEZING

Warm up your autumn with these gently spiced scones, which are incredibly simple to bake. If you don't already have all of the individual ground spices, consider purchasing a mixed spice blend, and use 1½–2 teaspoons for this recipe. Delicious served warm with lashings of vegan butter, blackcurrant jam, or a simple drizzle of maple syrup.

½ tsp ground cinnamon

½ tsp grated nutmeg

¼ tsp ground ginger

¼ tsp ground cardamom

¼ tsp ground cloves

pinch of ground allspice

220g (1⅔ cups) self-raising flour, plus 2 tbsp for dusting

1 tsp baking powder

2 tbsp caster (superfine) sugar

50g (1¾oz) chilled vegan butter

50g (1¾oz) sultanas (golden raisins)

120ml (½ cup) sweetened soya milk, plus 2 tsp for brushing

1 Preheat the oven to 220°C/425°F/gas mark 7. Line a baking tray with baking parchment.

2 In a large bowl, stir together the cinnamon, nutmeg, ginger, cardamom, cloves and allspice. Stir in the flour, baking powder and sugar and mix until the spices are evenly combined.

3 Rub in the butter until the mixture resembles fine breadcrumbs. Stir in the sultanas until coated in the flour mix.

4 Pour in the soya milk, a little at a time, and work into a thick, smooth dough.

5 Dust a clean work surface and your hands with flour and remove the dough from the bowl. Use your hands to press out the dough to a 2cm (¾in) thickness (no need to use a rolling pin). Use a scone cutter to press through the dough, avoiding any twisting of the cutter as this can distort the shape of the scone during cooking.

6 Place the scones on the lined baking tray and brush the tops of the scones with a little soya milk. Bake in the oven for 10–12 minutes until golden.

Speedy Tip

These scones will last for up to 4 days in a sealed container when stored in a cool, dry place. They can also be frozen to enjoy another time.

30

MINUTES

BREAKFAST BERRY CHARLOTTE

SERVES 4

Turn dessert into breakfast with this fruity, hearty dish. Sliced raisin and cinnamon loaf can be found in most supermarkets, and is not only perfect for toasting, but for using in this homely breakfast.

500g (4–5 cups/Ilb 2oz) mixed blackberries, raspberries, blueberries and strawberries, roughly chopped

2 tbsp fresh orange juice

2 tbsp maple syrup

I tbsp vegan butter

8 slices of raisin and cinnamon loaf

I tbsp flaked almonds

4 tbsp thick coconut yogurt, to serve

1 Preheat the oven to 200°C/400°F/gas mark 6.

2 Arrange the chopped fruit in a roasting dish and spoon over the orange juice and maple syrup. Loosely cover with foil and roast in the oven for 10 minutes.

3 Meanwhile, butter the slices of raisin and cinnamon loaf and quarter each slice into triangles.

4 Carefully remove the dish from the oven and lay the triangles over the fruit to cover the dish. Scatter over the flaked almonds, loosely cover with the foil and return to the oven for a further 10 minutes.

5 Carefully discard the foil and bake for a further 5 minutes, uncovered, until the triangles are golden and the fruit is bubbling around the sides.

6 Remove from the oven and spoon into dishes. Serve with a spoonful of coconut yogurt.

Speedy Tip

If you don't have fresh berries available, frozen fruit works well. Simply defrost mixed summer fruits, cherries or raspberries until thawed and cook as above.

AUBERGINE SHAKSHUKA WITH CHILLI YOGURT

SERVES 4 · SUITABLE FOR FREEZING (BEFORE ADDING THE YOGURT)

Smoky, sweet aubergine and peppers are simmered in a vegan-friendly version of the Middle Eastern breakfast classic. If serving more people or for extra protein, add in a can of drained and rinsed chickpeas (garbanzo beans). Serve with wedges of toasted pitta bread.

I tbsp sunflower oil

I aubergine (eggplant), roughly diced

I red onion, finely chopped

I red (bell) pepper, roughly chopped

2 garlic cloves, crushed

I tsp smoked paprika

pinch of mild chilli powder

2 tsp harissa paste

500g (2 cups/I7oz) passata (sieved tomatoes)

I tsp granulated sugar

4 tbsp soya yogurt

generous pinch of dried chilli flakes

generous pinch of sea salt and black pepper

juice of ½ unwaxed lemon

handful of coriander (cilantro) leaves, roughly torn

1 Heat the oil in a large pan, add the aubergine and cook over a high heat for 2 minutes, then add the red onion and pepper and soften for a further 2 minutes.

2 Stir in the garlic, smoked paprika, chilli powder and harissa and cook for a further minute, coating the vegetables in the spices.

3 Pour in the passata and stir in the sugar. Cook for 20 minutes over a medium-high heat, stirring frequently to avoid sticking.

4 Meanwhile, stir together the soya yogurt and chilli flakes in a bowl. Allow to infuse for a few minutes while the shakshuka is cooking.

5 Remove the pan from the heat and season to taste with salt and pepper. Stir through the lemon juice and scatter over the coriander leaves.

6 Spoon into serving bowls, then add a spoonful of the chilli yogurt over the top. Scatter over a few extra chilli flakes before serving, if you like.

Speedy Tip

Cook the aubergine, onion and pepper the evening before and keep them refrigerated in a sealed tub, for a speedier brunch the next morning.

BANANA, MAPLE AND BLUEBERRY BAKED OATS

SERVES 2 · SUITABLE FOR FREEZING

Start your day with some all-American flavours! These baked oats are simple to make, and cosy to eat. Serve with a spoonful of vegan yogurt, or smooth peanut butter.

1 ripe banana, mashed

2 tbsp maple syrup

200ml (generous ¾ cup) sweetened soya milk

pinch of ground cinnamon

100g (1 cup) rolled oats

generous handful of blueberries

handful of pecans, roughly chopped

1 Preheat the oven to 180°C/350°F/gas mark 4.

2 In a bowl, stir together the mashed banana, maple syrup, soya milk and cinnamon until combined.

3 Stir in the oats, blueberries and pecans until coated in the banana mixture.

4 Transfer to a small baking dish, then bake in the oven for 25 minutes until set and golden. Enjoy hot.

Speedy Tip

This simple breakfast cooks in under 30 minutes, but it can also be cooked the evening before, refrigerated and heated in the microwave the following day. It can also be frozen in portions – just make sure you defrost fully before reheating.

CHEESE, SPINACH AND CHIVE MUFFIN FRITTATAS

MAKES 6 · SUITABLE FOR FREEZING

These bite-sized frittatas are as cute as they are delicious. I prefer to use cream cheese for the perfect flavour balance with chives – mild and creamy but with a herby tang. Perfect served with a Bloody Mary.

½ tsp sunflower oil

280g (10oz) extra-firm tofu, drained and blotted (see Speedy Tip)

2 rounded tbsp vegan cream cheese

¼ tsp ground turmeric

1 tbsp soya milk

handful of fresh spinach leaves, thinly sliced

generous handful of chives, very finely chopped

generous pinch of sea salt and black pepper

1   Preheat the oven to 200°C/400°F/gas mark 6. Brush six holes of a muffin tray with a little sunflower oil.

2   Break the tofu up into a high-powered blender jug or food processor, then spoon in the cream cheese, turmeric and soya milk. Add 3 tablespoons of cold water and blitz on high, then add another 3 tablespoons of cold water and blitz again to form a thick paste (it should be thick enough to spoon rather than pour). Stir through the sliced spinach and chives and season with salt and plenty of pepper.

3   Spoon 2 tablespoons of the mix into each hole of the muffin tray.

4   Bake in the oven for 15 minutes, then reduce the heat to 180°C/350°F/gas mark 4 and bake for a further 5–7 minutes until the frittatas appear set. Remove from the oven and allow to stand for a few minutes before removing from the tray.

Speedy Tip

There's no need to press the tofu for this recipe; simply drain the tofu of excess moisture by patting with kitchen paper for a few minutes, and the tofu is ready to use.

BLACK BEAN BREAKFAST BURRITOS

SERVES 4

I love a savoury breakfast, especially one that lets the oven do all of the hard work! The Mexican-inspired filling is substantial and smoky with red onion, peppers and black beans. I spoon in some speedy shop-bought salsa, but feel free to make your own with tomatoes, red onion, coriander, lime juice and sea salt.

I sweet potato, peeled and cut into 2cm (¾in) cubes

I yellow (bell) pepper, thinly sliced

I green (bell) pepper, thinly sliced

I red onion, sliced

2 tbsp sunflower oil

2 tsp chipotle paste (ensure vegan)

pinch of dried chilli flakes

I x 400g (14oz) can of black beans, drained and rinsed

4 soft tortilla wraps, warmed

I large avocado, sliced

4 small handfuls of baby spinach leaves

4 tbsp tomato salsa

small handful of flat-leaf parsley, finely chopped

squeeze of juice from an unwaxed lime

generous pinch of smoked sea salt

1 Preheat the oven to 200°C/400°F/gas mark 6.

2 Arrange the sweet potato, peppers and onion in a deep baking tray (it's okay for these to overlap as they will cook by steaming in the oven).

3 In a small bowl, whisk together the sunflower oil, chipotle paste and chilli flakes. Drizzle over the vegetables and loosely cover with foil.

4 Bake for 15 minutes, then carefully remove from the oven, discard the foil and tip in the black beans. Stir to distribute and return to the oven to bake for a further 10 minutes, uncovered.

5 Warm the tortillas in the oven for a couple of minutes, then place on serving plates. Add a handful of spinach leaves and some avocado slices to each, with a spoonful of tomato salsa.

6 Remove the baking tray from the oven and scatter over the parsley. Stir through the lime juice and season with smoked sea salt, then spoon the mix into the wraps and fold. Serve hot.

Speedy Tip

Chipotle paste is a super-convenient ingredient and can be found in most supermarkets. It will last for 6–8 weeks in the fridge and can be used in smoky chipotle mac and cheese (page 176), or added to any chilli or fajitas for a burst of flavour with minimal effort.

LENTIL, POTATO AND ROSEMARY SOUP

SERVES 4 · SUITABLE FOR FREEZING

This simple soup is a firm favourite in my kitchen. Let it bubble away, thickening as it goes, before blitzing it into a silky soup that is perfect for lunch, with some crusty bread and vegan butter. Use fresh rosemary in this soup for the freshest fragrance and flavour.

1.5 litres (6 cups) hot vegetable stock

300g (1½ cups) dried red lentils, rinsed

2 baking potatoes, peeled and diced

4 carrots, peeled and chopped

2 onions, chopped

1 celery stick, roughly chopped

2 sprigs of fresh rosemary

generous pinch of sea salt and black pepper

1　Bring the vegetable stock to the boil in a large pan set over a medium-high heat, then add the lentils, potatoes, carrots, onions, celery and rosemary. Loosely cover the pan with a lid and cook for 25 minutes, stirring occasionally, until the potatoes have softened.

2　Remove and discard the tough rosemary stalks (leave in the rosemary leaves if they have broken off). Carefully pour the mixture into a jug blender and blitz until smooth.

3　Season to taste with salt and plenty of pepper.

Speedy Tip

If you prefer the final result a little thinner, simply add a few more tablespoons of water or vegetable stock.

MARMALADE SAUSAGE SANDWICHES WITH ROASTED ONIONS AND BLACKBERRY PICKLE

SERVES 2

This is the ultimate sausage sandwich – perfect for autumn with seasonal blackberries cooked until jammy in a sweet and tangy quick pickle. Brushing vegan sausages with marmalade gives them a new depth of flavour – the perfect match with roasted onions and pickle.

4 frozen vegan sausages

1 tbsp thick-cut orange marmalade

1 red onion, thinly sliced

1 tsp sunflower oil

50g (1¾oz) fresh blackberries, roughly chopped

pinch of caster (superfine) sugar

2 tsp cider vinegar

generous pinch of sea salt and black pepper

4 thick slices of white bread

2 tsp vegan butter

1   Preheat the oven to 180°C/350°F/gas mark 4.

2   Lay the sausages on a baking tray and use a pastry brush to sweep the marmalade over them. Place the onion slices on the same baking tray and drizzle with sunflower oil. Bake in the oven for 20–22 minutes until the sausages are golden and bubbling, and the onion is gently roasted.

3   Meanwhile, prepare the blackberry pickle. Place the blackberries and sugar in a pan and cook over a medium heat for 10–12 minutes until bubbling, pressing the blackberries with a wooden spoon to release the juices until they become jammy. Stir in the cider vinegar and season with salt and pepper.

4   Lay the bread on a clean work surface and butter one side of each slice.

5   Carefully remove the sausages and roasted onions from the oven and place two sausages in each sandwich, along with a scoop of roasted onions. Generously spoon over the blackberry pickle and place the remaining slices of bread on top. Slice the sandwiches and enjoy while hot.

Speedy Tip

Use your favourite brand of vegan sausages in the sandwich, and follow the cooking instructions on the packet. Marmalade sausages work best when they are cooked in the oven, so opt for oven-cook friendly brands (instead of the pan or grill, where the marmalade will burn).

TOMATO, BEAN AND PASTA SOUP

SERVES 4 · SUITABLE FOR FREEZING

This comforting, hearty soup makes the perfect lunch, as the combination of beans and pasta will keep you fuelled all afternoon. Toss over a few croutons, or serve with crusty bread and vegan butter.

I tbsp sunflower oil

I onion, diced

I carrot, peeled and diced

I celery stick, diced

2 stalks of cavolo nero, roughly chopped, tough stems discarded

I garlic clove, crushed

I tsp dried oregano

½ tsp dried mixed herbs

I x 400g (14oz) can of good-quality chopped tomatoes

I litre (4 cups) hot vegetable stock

80g (2¾oz) small dried pasta, such as stelline, farfalle, orzo, margheritine (ensure egg-free)

I x 400g (14oz) can of cannellini beans, drained and rinsed

generous pinch of sea salt and black pepper

small handful of flat-leaf parsley, chopped or torn

1 Heat the oil in a large pan, add the onion, carrot, celery and cavolo nero and cook over a medium heat for 3–4 minutes, stirring frequently. Next, add the garlic, oregano and mixed herbs and cook for a further minute.

2 Pour in the chopped tomatoes and vegetable stock and bring to the boil.

3 When the liquid is simmering, add the pasta and cannellini beans. Cook for 15 minutes until the pasta is al dente. Stir occasionally to avoid sticking.

4 Remove from the heat and season with salt and plenty of pepper. Scatter with parsley just before serving.

Speedy Tip

Choose small, shaped pasta that sits easily on a soup spoon for this recipe. My favourites are stelline or margheritine, but orzo, macaroni or farfalle work well too.

SWEET CHILLI CAULIFLOWER WITH CRUNCHY SLAW

SERVES 4

A dish light enough for lunch that doesn't fail on flavour or fun! Aim for the cauliflower florets to be as evenly sized as possible to ensure they cook at the same time. Many brands of sweet chilli sauce available in supermarkets are vegan-friendly, but always check the label as some may contain fish.

5 tbsp sweet chilli sauce (ensure vegan)

½ tsp dark soy sauce

I cauliflower, broken into florets

2 tbsp sesame seeds

2 carrots, peeled and grated

I green apple, grated

½ small red cabbage, finely shredded

2 spring onions (scallions), finely sliced

generous handful of coriander (cilantro) leaves, roughly torn

I rounded tbsp thick coconut yogurt

juice of ½ unwaxed lime

1 Preheat the oven to 200°C/400°F/gas mark 6.

2 In a small bowl, mix together the sweet chilli sauce and soy sauce. Use a pastry brush to generously sweep the mix over the cauliflower florets and place on a baking tray.

3 Bake in the oven for 15 minutes, then carefully remove the baking tray from the oven and use tongs to turn the florets. Scatter with sesame seeds then return to the oven for a further 10 minutes.

4 Meanwhile, make the slaw. In a bowl, stir together the grated carrots, apple, cabbage, spring onions (reserving a few pieces of spring onion for garnish later) and coriander. Stir in the coconut yogurt and lime juice and combine. Spoon the slaw onto serving dishes.

5 Remove the cauliflower florets from the oven and place them over the slaw. Scatter with the remaining spring onion pieces. Serve hot.

Speedy Tip

The slaw will last for up to 2 days in the fridge, and is also delicious with tempura, stir-fries or rice pop tofu with katsu sauce (page 197).

WARM ASPARAGUS, POTATO AND TOMATO SALAD

SERVES 2

This simple salad is perfect for cool spring lunches, with seasonal new potatoes and asparagus. Choose mixed colour/variety baby tomatoes for vibrancy if you can, but if you can only source baby red tomatoes, choose the ripest and glossiest ones for the best flavour.

8 new potatoes, halved

250g (9oz) fine asparagus tips, any woody stems discarded

2 tbsp extra virgin olive oil

juice of ½ unwaxed lemon

generous pinch of sea salt and black pepper

small handful of flat-leaf parsley, very finely chopped

2 handfuls of wild rocket (arugula)

8 mixed baby tomatoes, sliced

handful of small basil leaves

1 Bring a pan of water to the boil over a high heat, then add the new potatoes. Boil for 15 minutes.

2 Add the asparagus to the same pan as the potatoes and cook for a further 5–6 minutes until tender.

3 Meanwhile, in a small bowl, whisk together the olive oil, lemon juice, salt and pepper. Stir through the parsley and set aside.

4 Toss the rocket and tomatoes into bowls or onto a serving platter.

5 Drain the water from the pan and place the potatoes and asparagus on top of the rocket and tomatoes. Spoon over the dressing and scatter over the basil leaves. Serve warm.

Speedy Tip

This simple salad is fresh and light, but for more substance serve with a handful of cooked broad beans, butterbeans or toasted pine nuts.

BLACK PEPPER CRACKERS

SERVES 4

Sometimes, you just need a snacky lunch of crackers, vegan cheese and a spoonful of chutney. These simple crackers have the perfect balance of freshly cracked black pepper and sea salt. Crisp, golden and worth the extra effort.

150g (1¼ cups) plain (all-purpose) flour

¼ tsp cracked black pepper (about 6 turns on a pepper mill)

1 tsp sea salt, plus extra for finishing

½ tsp caster (superfine) sugar

2 tbsp sunflower oil

1   Preheat the oven to 200°C/400°F/gas mark 7.

2   Stir together the flour, black pepper, sea salt and sugar in a bowl.

3   Make a well in the centre of the mixture and spoon in the oil and 70g (2½oz) of cold water. Use your hands to bring together into a dough.

4   Lay out a piece of baking parchment and use a rolling pin to roll the dough to a thickness of 5mm (¼in). Sprinkle with a generous pinch of sea salt and gently push the flakes in. Use a sharp knife to slice the crackers into bite-sized squares or diamonds.

5   Transfer the parchment to a baking tray and bake in the oven for 12–15 minutes until lightly golden. Allow to cool for at least 10 minutes to crisp up.

Speedy Tip
These crackers will keep for up to a week in a sealed container, stored in a cool place.

APRICOT, LEMON AND HERB PILAF

SERVES 4

Some lunches are made to be special, and made to be shared. This rice pilaf is summery and fresh, and is a welcome addition to any weekend al fresco lunch. Serve warm as a sharing plate, or refrigerate and serve cold with salad leaves as a lighter lunch.

I tbsp sunflower oil

I onion, chopped

I tsp ground turmeric

½ tsp ground cumin

I tsp harissa paste

250g (1¼ cups) basmati rice

800ml (3⅓ cups) hot vegetable stock

100g (3½oz) good-quality dried apricots, roughly chopped

2 rounded tbsp flaked almonds

zest and juice of I unwaxed lemon

generous handful of flat-leaf parsley, finely chopped

handful of fresh dill, finely chopped

generous pinch of sea salt and black pepper

1 In a large pan, heat the oil and onion over a medium-high heat for 2–3 minutes until softened. Stir in the turmeric, cumin and harissa paste and cook for a further minute.

2 Pour in the rice and vegetable stock, and bring to the boil. Reduce the heat to medium and simmer for 15 minutes, stirring frequently to avoid sticking, until the liquid has been absorbed.

3 Remove from the heat and use a fork to work through the rice, separating the grains. Stir in the dried apricots, then place a lid on the pan and stand for 5 minutes.

4 Meanwhile, add the flaked almonds to a dry, flat pan and toast for 2–3 minutes unto golden and fragrant.

5 Stir the lemon zest and juice, parsley and dill through the rice until evenly distributed. Season to taste with salt and pepper, then scatter over the toasted almonds.

Speedy Tip

White basmati rice has a wonderful aroma and flavour, and it also cooks much more quickly than long grain or wild rice.

167

CREAMY PEANUT NOODLE SOUP

SERVES 4 · SUITABLE FOR FREEZING

This addictively slippery soup is gently spiced with Eastern flavours, creamy coconut milk and soft noodles. Best eaten with a spoon and chopsticks, or a spork, for the perfect lunch.

I tbsp sunflower oil

Icm (½in) piece of ginger, grated

pinch of dried chilli flakes

I carrot, peeled and thinly sliced into half-rounds

4 sugarsnap peas, sliced lengthways

I tbsp red Thai curry paste (ensure vegan)

I x 400ml (I4fl oz) can of full-fat coconut milk

2 rounded tbsp smooth peanut butter

300g (I0oz) soft ready-to-wok noodles (ensure vegan)

2 tsp light soy sauce

I spring onion (scallion), finely sliced

small handful of coriander (cilantro) leaves

juice of ½ unwaxed lime

1   Heat the oil in a large pan, add the ginger, chilli flakes, carrot and sugarsnap peas and cook over a medium-high heat for 2–3 minutes until the vegetables begin to soften.

2   Stir in the curry paste, then pour in the coconut milk along with 250ml (I cup) of hot water. Stir in the peanut butter and simmer for I5 minutes.

3   Add the noodles and gently stir to separate. Simmer for a further 5–6 minutes until the noodles are coated in the soup base and are piping hot.

4   Remove from the heat and stir in the soy sauce. Scatter with spring onion and coriander, then squeeze over the lime juice. Serve hot.

Speedy Tip

Soft, ready-to-wok noodles are found in the ambient section of most supermarkets and they are unlikely to contain egg, but always check the ingredients before you buy. The soft noodles found in supermarket chiller sections are more likely to contain eggs.

SPICY POTATO AND PEA WRAPS

SERVES 2 · SUITABLE FOR FREEZING (POTATO AND PEA FILLING)

Filling, warming and spiced, these wraps make a substantial and flavoursome lunch. This recipe is a great way to use up any remaining new potatoes from the bag, alongside store cupboard staples. The waxy texture of the new potato carries the spice, with pops of freshness from the peas. Serve either hot or cold.

5 new potatoes, halved

2 tbsp sunflower oil

I red onion, thinly sliced

I garlic clove, crushed

½ tsp mustard seeds

pinch of dried chilli flakes

I tsp garam masala

½ tsp ground turmeric

4 tbsp frozen peas

2 naan breads (ensure vegan)

small handful of coriander (cilantro), roughly torn

pinch of sea salt

2 tbsp thick coconut yogurt

2 tsp mango chutney

1   Bring a pan of water to the boil over a medium-high heat, then add the new potatoes and cook for 20 minutes until softened.

2   In a separate flat pan, add the oil, onion, garlic, mustard seeds and chilli flakes. Cook over a medium heat for 4–5 minutes until the onion has softened. Stir in the garam masala and turmeric until combined. Add the frozen peas and cook for 2–3 minutes until defrosted.

3   Meanwhile, warm the naan breads: sprinkle the breads with a few drops of water and put an oven preheated to 180°C/350°F/gas 4 for 5 minutes, or in the microwave for 10 seconds.

4   Drain the potatoes and then add them to the flat pan and roughly crush down, coating in the spiced oil. Remove the pan from the heat and scatter over the coriander and sea salt.

5   Lay out the warmed naan breads on serving plates and spoon in the spiced potatoes and pea mix. Spoon over the coconut yogurt and mango chutney, then fold the naan bread to contain the filling.

Speedy Tip

Some brands of shop-bought naan bread contain milk, but many supermarket own brands are accidentally vegan so always check the label before you buy. If you don't have naan breads available, soft tortilla wraps are an excellent substitute, particularly the garlic and coriander varieties.

GOLDEN QUINOA SALAD

SERVES 4

Quinoa is easy to cook and delicious to eat in this Californian-style salad with dried apricots, cranberries and avocados. I love cooking quinoa with a pinch of ground turmeric for a golden colour, which looks luxurious with the jewel-like dried fruits and herbs.

200g (1 cup) quinoa

pinch of ground turmeric

2 rounded tbsp flaked almonds

100g (3½oz) good-quality dried apricots, diced

2 rounded tbsp dried cranberries

2 generous tbsp tahini

1 tbsp soya yogurt

drizzle of extra virgin olive oil

pinch of sea salt

juice of 1 unwaxed lemon

handful of flat-leaf parsley, finely chopped

small handful of mint leaves, finely chopped, plus extra leaves to serve

1 large avocado, sliced

2 baby gem lettuces, sliced into wedges, tough core discarded

1   Add the quinoa and turmeric to a large pan and pour in enough cold water to cover it. Bring to the boil over a high heat, then reduce the heat to medium and simmer for 15 minutes.

2   In another dry pan, add the flaked almonds and toast for 2–3 minutes until golden and fragrant. Set aside.

3   Remove the pan with the golden quinoa from the heat. Drain any excess liquid from the quinoa and stir in the dried apricots and cranberries. Cover the pan with a lid and leave to stand for 10 minutes.

4   Meanwhile, make the dressing by whisking together the tahini, soya yogurt, olive oil and sea salt.

5   Remove the lid from the pan and stir in the lemon juice, parsley and mint. Stir in the sliced avocado and toasted almonds.

6   Arrange the lettuce wedges on serving plates, then spoon over the quinoa mix. Drizzle generously with the tahini dressing and scatter with mint leaves.

Speedy Tip
This salad is delicious served either warm or cold. If serving cold, the salad will last for up to 3 days in the fridge in a sealed container.

AUBERGINE AND LENTIL CURRY

SERVES 4 GENEROUSLY · SUITABLE FOR FREEZING

This comforting dish is simple but delicious, and a great way to enjoy aubergines. There's no need to salt aubergines before use, simply slice into even wedges and cook in a hot pan until they begin to soften. The aubergines will take on the lightly spiced flavour of the curry, and give a meaty bite to this dish. Serve with a generous swirl of thick, coconut yogurt and basmati rice.

I tbsp sunflower oil

I aubergine (eggplant), sliced into 5cm (2in) wedges

I onion, diced

2 garlic cloves, crushed

I tsp ground cumin

I tsp ground turmeric

pinch of dried chilli flakes

2 rounded tbsp mild curry paste (ensure vegan)

250g (I¼ cups) dried red lentils

I.5 litres (6 cups) hot vegetable stock

juice of I unwaxed lemon

generous pinch of sea salt and black pepper

small handful of coriander (cilantro) leaves, roughly torn

1 Heat the oil in a large pan, add the aubergine and cook over a high heat for 2 minutes, then add the onion and cook for a further 2 minutes, stirring continuously to cook the aubergine evenly.

2 Stir in the garlic until combined, then add the cumin, turmeric and chilli flakes and cook for a further minute.

3 Stir in the curry paste until the aubergine and onion are coated, then add the lentils and vegetable stock. Cook over a high heat for 15 minutes, stirring frequently; when the lentils start to break down, reduce the heat slightly and cook for a further 10 minutes until thickened.

4 Remove from the heat and stir through the lemon juice. Season to taste with salt and pepper. Scatter with coriander leaves just before serving.

Speedy Tip

Stir the curry frequently to help break up the red lentils. Not only will this reduce the cooking time, but it will result in a creamier curry.

SMOKY CHIPOTLE MAC AND CHEESE

SERVES 2 · SUITABLE FOR FREEZING (CHIPOTLE CHEESE SAUCE)

Savoury, smoky and creamy, this twist on mac and cheese is warming and comforting. Cream cheese adds to the silky, creamy texture of the sauce, but grated vegan hard cheese also works well if you only have that available. Don't skip the chives – they add a gentle, garlicky flavour that brings this mac and cheese together.

3 carrots, peeled and roughly chopped

1 large baking potato, peeled and roughly chopped

½ small butternut squash, peeled and roughly chopped

1 yellow (bell) pepper, roughly chopped

200g (7oz) dried macaroni (ensure egg-free)

2 rounded tbsp vegan cream cheese

1 tbsp chipotle paste (ensure vegan)

½ tsp smoked paprika

½ tsp dried oregano

200ml (generous ¾ cup) soya milk

generous pinch of smoked sea salt and black pepper

generous handful of chives, finely chopped

1   Bring a large pan of water to the boil over a medium-high heat, then throw in the chopped carrots, potato, butternut squash and yellow pepper. Simmer for 20 minutes until the vegetables have softened, then drain away the water.

2   Meanwhile, bring another pan of water to the boil and throw in the macaroni. Cook for 10–12 minutes until al dente, then drain away the water. Return the cooked macaroni to the pan.

3   Add the cooked carrot, potato, butternut squash and yellow pepper to a high-powered blender jug and spoon in the cream cheese, chipotle paste, paprika and oregano. Pour in the soya milk and blitz until completely smooth. Season to taste with smoked sea salt and black pepper.

4   Pour the sauce over the macaroni and stir through over a medium heat.

5   Remove from the heat and stir in the chives before serving in bowls.

Speedy Tip

Frozen butternut squash is available from supermarkets, and works just as well in place of fresh butternut squash.

HEARTY COBBLER WITH CHIVE DUMPLINGS

SERVES 2 · SUITABLE FOR FREEZING

This supper is warming and filling: the rustic baked chive dumplings are almost like savoury scones, which beautifully soak up the rich juices from the cobbler filling. Make the base filling in a hob-to-table pot, then serve the baked dumplings over the top, and enjoy the supper family-style.

For the chive dumplings

160g (1¼ cups) self-raising flour, plus extra for rolling

generous handful of chives, finely chopped

generous pinch of dried rosemary

pinch of salt

50g (1¾oz) vegan butter

100ml (scant ½ cup) soya milk, plus 2 tsp for glazing

For the filling

1 tbsp sunflower oil

1 leek, finely chopped

1 carrot, peeled and finely chopped into half-rounds

1 celery stick, thinly sliced

generous glug of red wine (ensure vegan)

generous handful of shredded kale, tough stems removed

1 x 400g (14oz) can of chopped tomatoes

1 x 400g (14oz) can of green lentils, drained and rinsed

2 dried bay leaves

1 sprig of fresh rosemary

generous pinch of sea salt and black pepper

1   Preheat the oven to 200°C/400°F/gas mark 6 and line a baking tray with baking parchment.

2   In a bowl, stir together the flour, chives, rosemary and salt. Rub in the butter with your fingers until the mixture begins to resemble breadcrumbs. Stir in the soya milk to form a dough.

3   Sprinkle a clean work surface with flour and flatten the dough roughly to a thickness of about 2.5cm (1in). Use a scone cutter to cut out 8 dumplings and place them on the baking tray. Brush with a little soya milk, then bake in the oven for 10–12 minutes until light golden.

4   While the dumplings are baking, prepare the filling. Heat the oil in a large hob-to-table pot, add the leek, carrot and celery and cook over a medium-high heat for 4 minutes, stirring often. Pour in the red wine and reduce for 1 minute.

5   Add the kale, chopped tomatoes and lentils, stir, then add the bay leaves and rosemary. Cook for 15 minutes over a high heat, stirring frequently to avoid sticking.

6   Remove the pot from the heat and discard the bay leaves and rosemary sprig. Season to taste with salt and pepper.

7   Remove the baked dumplings from the oven and place over the filling just before serving.

Speedy Tip

Freeze the filling and the chive dumplings separately, then assemble after reheating to keep both elements at their best.

ALLOTMENT TART

SERVES 4

This light and summery supper is as simple as it is delicious, and is always popular when served at a barbecue or garden party! Any leftovers are perfect for lunch the following day. Serve with a leafy salad and crispy potato slices.

1 garlic clove, bruised

2 courgettes (zucchini), thinly sliced into rounds

1 red onion, sliced into rings

2 beef tomatoes, sliced into rounds

1 yellow (bell) pepper, sliced into rounds

drizzle of sunflower oil

pinch of dried oregano

pinch of dried mixed herbs

1 sheet of ready-rolled puff pastry (ensure vegan)

drizzle of extra virgin olive oil

generous pinch of sea salt and black pepper

small handful of basil leaves

1   Preheat the oven to 190°C/375°F/gas mark 5.

2   Rub the garlic clove over the inside of a deep baking tray. Lay the sliced courgettes, onion, tomatoes and pepper in the tray (it's okay if they overlap). Drizzle with sunflower oil and scatter over the oregano and mixed herbs. Roast in the oven for 25 minutes.

3   Lay the pastry sheet on another baking tray and carefully fold in the edges by 1cm (½in). Rub the centre section with the garlic clove and pierce a few times with a fork. Bake in the oven for 10–12 minutes until golden and risen.

4   Remove the roasted vegetables and pastry sheet from the oven. Press the centre of the puff pastry down, and lay the vegetables within the tart.

5   Drizzle with a little extra virgin olive oil and season with sea salt and plenty of black pepper. Scatter with basil leaves just before serving.

Speedy Tip

Many brands of shop-bought puff pastry are suitable for vegans as vegetable oil is used instead of dairy butter, but always read the ingredients before you buy.

SPICY PEPPER, RED BEAN AND ORANGE RICE POT

SERVES 4

This all-in-one supper is perfect for those evenings when you don't have time for a lot of washing up, but you need something warming, zesty and substantial. Delicious bowl food for any season.

250g (1¼ cups) basmati rice

1 tsp smoked paprika

½ tsp ground turmeric

800ml (3⅓ cups) hot vegetable stock

1 red (bell) pepper, roughly chopped

6 cherry tomatoes, halved

1 x 400g (14oz) can of red kidney beans, drained and rinsed

1 unwaxed orange

juice of 1 unwaxed lemon

generous handful of flat-leaf parsley, finely chopped

handful of chives, finely chopped

handful of coriander (cilantro), roughly torn

generous pinch of sea salt

1 red chilli, thinly sliced (optional)

1   Add the rice, smoked paprika and turmeric to a large pan and pour in the vegetable stock. Bring to the boil over a medium-high heat, then add the pepper, cherry tomatoes and kidney beans. Simmer for 15 minutes, stirring frequently to avoid sticking.

2   Use a sharp knife to remove all the peel and pith from the orange, then slice widthways into circles.

3   Remove the pan from the heat and stir in the orange slices and lemon juice. Add the lid to the pan and allow it to stand for 10 minutes.

4   Fork through to fluff up the rice and then season to taste with sea salt and stir in red chilli, if you like. Top with the parsley, chives and coriander before serving.

Speedy Tip

Omit or reduce the sliced red chilli if you prefer a milder dish, or when serving to children. Be generous with the fresh parsley, chives and coriander, for freshness and zing.

AUTUMN TRAYBAKE

SERVES 2

Imagine a cosy autumn evening: it's cold outside and toasty inside. A fragrant all-in-one traybake is roasting in the oven, with earthy mushrooms, jammy figs, sweet potato and crunchy pine nuts. It doesn't get much better than this. Delicious served as a complete meal-in-a-bowl, or with steamed cavolo nero and broccoli.

I garlic clove, bruised

250g (9oz) chestnut mushrooms, brushed clean and halved

I sweet potato, peeled and cut into chunks

2 red onions, peeled and cut into wedges

2 figs, quartered

drizzle of sunflower oil

pinch of dried sage

2 sprigs of fresh rosemary

2 tbsp pine nuts

small handful of flat-leaf parsley, finely chopped

generous pinch of sea salt and black pepper

1   Preheat the oven to 190°C/375°F/gas mark 5.

2   Rub the garlic clove over a deep roasting tray to release the fragrance, then discard.

3   Add the mushrooms, sweet potato, red onions and figs to the roasting tray. Drizzle with sunflower oil and stir to lightly coat the vegetables. Sprinkle over the sage, and lay in the whole rosemary sprigs. Roast in the oven for 20 minutes.

4   Carefully remove from the oven and scatter over the pine nuts. Return to the oven for a further 5 minutes until golden.

5   Remove from the oven and stir through the parsley. Season to taste with salt and pepper.

Speedy Tip

Cut the sweet potato into even chunks, approximately 2cm (¾in) in size, to ensure even cooking in under 30 minutes.

HARISSA CHICKPEA AND CAULIFLOWER ONE-POT

SERVES 4 · SUITABLE FOR FREEZING

Warming, fresh and simple, this one-pot is a regular in my kitchen as it is easy
to make and delicious to eat. Cauliflower is the star of the show, carrying
the gently spiced flavours with a little bite. Serve with bread or some simple
couscous, or blood orange, red cabbage and lentil salad (page 44).

I tbsp sunflower oil

I red onion, thinly sliced

2 garlic cloves, crushed

I tsp ground cumin

½ tsp ground turmeric

I tbsp harissa paste

I small cauliflower, broken
into bite-sized florets

200g (7oz) fine green
beans, trimmed

500g (2 cups/I7oz)
passata (sieved tomatoes)

I x 400g (I4oz) can of
chickpeas (garbanzo
beans), drained and rinsed

handful of good-quality
dried apricots, roughly
chopped

4 tbsp soya yogurt

squeeze of juice from an
unwaxed lemon

pinch of sea salt

handful of flat-leaf
parsley, torn

1   Heat the oil in a large pan, add the red onion and
    cook over a medium-high heat for 2 minutes until it
    begins to soften. Stir in the garlic, cumin, turmeric
    and harissa and cook for a further minute.

2   Add the cauliflower florets and green beans and
    stir to coat in the spices, then pour in the passata,
    chickpeas and apricots. Simmer for 25 minutes
    until the cauliflower is tender.

3   Meanwhile, stir together the soya yogurt, lemon
    juice and sea salt in a small bowl and set aside.

4   Remove the pan from the heat, season with a little
    salt and stir in the parsley.

5   Ladle into serving bowls and top with the salted
    lemon yogurt.

Speedy Tip

If you don't have chickpeas available, or fancy
an ingredient switch-up, butterbeans make a
wonderful alternative (especially the plumper
varieties that are sold in jars).

MAPLE-ROASTED SWEET POTATO TACOS

SERVES 4

If you're looking for a go-to Taco Tuesday recipe – you've just found it! This easy recipe combines sticky roasted sweet potatoes with crisp salad vegetables, creamy avocado and zesty lime. Crunchy taco shells are a fun contrast to the tender roasted sweet potatoes, or use soft wraps, if you prefer.

3 tbsp sunflower oil

3 tbsp maple syrup

½ tsp smoked paprika

pinch of dried chilli flakes

2 sweet potatoes, peeled and cut into 2cm (¾in) pieces

1 red onion, roughly sliced

8 crunchy taco shells

handful of iceberg lettuce, finely shredded

1 avocado, sliced

2 radishes, finely sliced

juice of ½ unwaxed lime

generous pinch of sea salt

1 Preheat the oven to 190°C/375°F/gas mark 5.

2 In a large bowl, whisk together the oil, maple syrup, smoked paprika and chilli flakes, then stir in the sweet potato and red onion. Stir to coat the vegetables then transfer into a deep roasting tray. Roast in the oven for 25 minutes until the sweet potato has softened.

3 Meanwhile, lay out the taco shells, and start filling with the lettuce, avocado and radishes.

4 Remove the roasting tray from the oven and spoon the sweet potatoes and roasted onion into the taco shells. Squeeze over the lime juice and sprinkle with sea salt. Serve hot.

Speedy Tip

Let the oven do the hard work for 25 minutes, while you prepare the taco extras of lettuce, avocado, radish and lime. Load each taco shell before serving, or lay it all out, family-style, for everyone to load themselves at the table.

CRISPY POPADOM BALTI PIE

SERVES 4

I used to make this spicy pie with vegan filo pastry, then one day, halfway into making the recipe, I realized that I had no filo pastry (it happens to us all!). I did have a pack of ready-to-eat popadoms at the back of the cupboard, some of which had been broken on the way home from the supermarket. So I topped the pie filling with roughly crushed popadoms – and it became an accidentally new and improved family favourite!

1 tbsp sunflower oil

1 onion, diced

1 carrot, peeled and chopped

8 small florets of cauliflower

1 yellow (bell) pepper, roughly chopped

2 garlic cloves, crushed

1 tsp ground turmeric

1 tsp ground cumin

¼ tsp dried chilli flakes

1 rounded tbsp mild curry paste (ensure vegan)

1 x 400g (14oz) can of chopped tomatoes

6 new potatoes, quartered

1 rounded tbsp frozen peas

handful of coriander (cilantro), roughly chopped

generous pinch of sea salt and black pepper

8 ready-to-eat popadoms, roughly broken up

1 Heat the oil in a large hob-to-table pot, add the onion, carrot, cauliflower and pepper and cook over a high heat for 2 minutes, stirring frequently.

2 Add the garlic, turmeric, cumin and chilli flakes and cook for a further minute until fragrant.

3 Spoon in the curry paste, then add the chopped tomatoes and potatoes. Simmer over a high heat for 20 minutes, stirring frequently, then stir in the peas and cook for a further 5 minutes.

4 Remove the pot from the hob and stir in the coriander and sea salt. Scatter over a generous layer of the broken popadoms and serve hot.

Speedy Tip
Chop the new potatoes into quarters to reduce the cooking time, or reduce the cooking time even more by using canned new potatoes that have been thoroughly rinsed. Canned new potatoes work very well in a dish like this, as they absorb the flavours well and still have a satisfying, waxy texture.

NOURISHING RICE BOWL

SERVES 2

I'm a huge fan of white basmati rice, for its quick-cook qualities and fragrance,
but from time to time, when I have a little longer to spend in the kitchen,
I cook up some short grain brown rice, which is nutty and earthy. This fresh
and fragrant dish is vibrant, nutritious and full of healthy foods.

150g (¾ cup) short grain brown rice

4 tbsp frozen edamame beans

I large carrot, peeled and grated or cut into julienne

4 radishes, thinly sliced

4cm (1½in) piece of cucumber, finely sliced

2 tsp sesame seeds

I avocado, thinly sliced

2 tsp pumpkin seeds

juice of I unwaxed lime

pinch of sea salt

small handful of coriander (cilantro), torn

1 Add the rice to a lidded pan and pour over 250ml (I cup) of boiling water. Bring to the boil over a high heat, then reduce the heat to medium and loosely cover with the lid. Simmer for 20 minutes, then remove from the heat. Secure the lid firmly and leave to stand for 5 minutes.

2 Meanwhile, add the edamame beans to a separate pan and cover with boiling water. Cook over a high heat for 3–4 minutes, then drain away the water and set aside.

3 Arrange the carrot, radishes, cucumber and edamame in serving bowls, leaving space for the rice once it has cooked.

4 Scatter sesame seeds over the sliced avocado and press them on to secure. Lay the slices in the bowls.

5 Stir the pumpkin seeds into the cooked rice and squeeze through the lime juice. Spoon into the bowls.

6 Season with salt and scatter with coriander.

Speedy Tip

I love to serve these while the rice is still hot, but they are equally delicious as a packed lunch, kept in the fridge until it's time to enjoy.

ALL IN ONE SPAGHETTI BOLOGNESE

SERVES 4 · SUITABLE FOR FREEZING

Forget two pans on spag bol night! This version is cooked up in one pan, which not only reduces your washing up, but by cooking the pasta in the bolognese sauce, creates a silky, comforting texture. A midweek winner that will become a family favourite! Serve with a simple rocket (arugula) salad, or a garlic baguette (French stick).

1 tbsp sunflower oil

1 onion, diced

1 carrot, peeled and diced

1 celery stick, diced

1 red (bell) pepper, diced

2 garlic cloves, crushed

1 tsp dried oregano

1 tsp dried mixed herbs

4 tbsp red wine (ensure vegan)

1 x 400g (14oz) can of green lentils, drained and rinsed

500g (2 cups/17oz) passata (sieved tomatoes)

600ml (2½ cups) hot vegetable stock

250g (9oz) dried spaghetti (ensure egg-free)

generous pinch of sea salt and black pepper

handful of small basil leaves

1 Heat the oil in a large pan, add the onion, carrot, celery and pepper and cook over a medium-high heat for 3 minutes, stirring frequently until the vegetables begin to soften.

2 Stir in the garlic, oregano and mixed herbs and cook for a further minute.

3 Pour in the red wine and reduce for 2 minutes.

4 Add the lentils, passata and vegetable stock and stir to combine. Cook for 10 minutes over a high heat, stirring frequently.

5 Add the spaghetti to the pan and cook for 10–12 minutes, pushing it further into the pan as it softens and cooks until it is fully submerged in the sauce.

6 Remove from the heat and stir gently to combine. Season to taste with salt and plenty of pepper. Scatter with basil just before serving.

Speedy Tip

Measure the liquid and weigh the dried pasta as accurately as possible, to allow perfect cooking of each element. The bolognese will initially have more sauce than a standard bolognese, but when the pasta is added, it will thicken up from the starches in the pasta.

FRYING PAN PIZZA

SERVES 2

No yeast, no time to knead and prove, no pizza oven? No problem! This pizza is made in a frying pan, with a fragrant sauce, melted vegan cheese and fresh basil. As you won't be using a large quantity of passata, opt for a jarred variety that you can seal ready for another recipe, or freeze the remaining pack. Great for camping, or warm days when you don't want to heat up the oven.

200g (1¾ cups) self-raising flour, plus extra for dusting

generous pinch of sea salt

2 tbsp extra virgin olive oil, plus extra for frying and drizzling

2 tbsp grated vegan hard cheese

For the pizza sauce

2 tsp sunflower oil

1 garlic clove, crushed

6 tbsp passata (sieved tomatoes)

4 cherry tomatoes, sliced

pinch of caster (superfine) sugar

handful of basil leaves, finely chopped, plus a few left whole to garnish

generous pinch of sea salt and black pepper

1   Heat the sunflower oil in a pan and add the garlic. Sauté over a medium heat for 1 minute until fragrant. Stir in the passata, tomatoes and sugar and simmer for 8 minutes, stirring frequently. Remove from the heat and stir in the chopped basil, then season with salt and pepper.

2   Stir the flour and salt together in a bowl. Make a well in the centre and add the olive oil, along with 5–6 tablespoons of lukewarm water, and mix into a soft dough that isn't too sticky.

3   Lightly dust a clean work surface with flour and roll the dough out to fit a (lidded) 20cm (8in) frying pan.

4   Drizzle a little olive oil in the frying pan and press in the dough. Cook over a medium heat, without the lid, for 9–10 minutes until golden.

5   Spoon over the tomato base sauce and scatter with the grated cheese. Place a lid over the pan and cook for 1–2 minutes until the cheese has melted.

6   Remove from the heat and scatter with basil leaves, and a little extra olive oil, sea salt and black pepper, if you like.

Speedy Tip

If you fancy some extra toppings but don't want to turn on the oven, try adding sliced, jarred antipasti vegetables, including sundried tomatoes, charred (bell) peppers, artichokes, olives... or even pineapple chunks!

RICE POP TOFU WITH KATSU SAUCE

SERVES 2 · SUITABLE FOR FREEZING (KATSU SAUCE)

Crispy rice pop cereal isn't just for breakfast – it makes a tasty and crunchy crumb for tofu. Katsu curry sauce is simple to make with a few store cupboard ingredients – the trick is to blitz until smooth in a high-powered blender for that familiar, silky texture. I like to serve this up with rice and something green.

3 rounded tbsp vegan mayonnaise

pinch of dried chilli flakes

grated zest of 1 unwaxed lime

drizzle of sunflower oil

8 rounded tbsp crispy rice pop-style cereal (ensure vegan, see tip)

280g (10oz) extra-firm tofu, drained and blotted, sliced horizontally into 3 slices, then each slice into 2cm (¾in) fingers

generous pinch of sea salt and black pepper

handful of coriander (cilantro) leaves, torn

wedges of unwaxed lime, to serve (optional)

For the katsu sauce

1 tbsp sunflower oil

1 onion, roughly diced

1 carrot, roughly chopped

2cm (¾in) piece of ginger, peeled and grated

2 garlic cloves, roughly sliced

3 tsp mild curry powder

1 x 400ml (14fl oz) can of coconut milk

1 tsp cornflour (cornstarch)

1 tsp maple syrup

1 tsp light soy sauce

1 Preheat the oven to 190°C/375°F/gas mark 5.

2 In a bowl, stir together the mayonnaise, chilli flakes, lime zest and sunflower oil.

3 Lay out the rice pop cereal on a plate. Dip each finger of tofu into the mayonnaise mix, then into the rice pop cereal, covering all surfaces. Lay on a baking tray and bake in the oven for 25 minutes until golden.

4 Meanwhile, make the curry sauce. Heat the sunflower oil in a wok over a high heat, then add the onion, carrot and ginger and stir-fry for 2–3 minutes until they begin to soften. Add the garlic and curry powder and cook for 1 further minute. Reduce the heat slightly and pour in the coconut milk and cornflour. Stir to combine and cook for 10 minutes, stirring frequently. Spoon in the maple syrup and soy sauce, stir, then remove from the heat. Transfer to a high-powered blender jug or food processor and blitz on high until completely smooth.

5 Remove the tofu from the oven and place on serving plates. Spoon over the katsu sauce just before serving and scatter with coriander. Serve with wedges of lime, if you like.

Speedy Tip

Some brands of rice pops contain vitamin D from an animal source (often sheep's wool), making the product unsuitable for vegans, but many supermarket own brands do not fortify using this source of vitamin D so always check the packet before you buy.

CRISPY SWEET POTATO TOPPED CHILLI

SERVES 4 · SUITABLE FOR FREEZING

Bored of serving chilli with rice? Switch it for crispy sweet potatoes, and lay them over the chilli, for a comforting chilli-hotpot hybrid. I love the mixture of red kidney beans and green lentils, but feel free use your favourite beans such as canned butterbeans or black beans, depending on what you have in the store cupboard. A new family classic!

2 large sweet potatoes, peeled and thinly sliced

drizzle of sunflower oil

I x 400g (I4oz) can of chopped tomatoes

I x 400g (I4oz) can of red kidney beans, drained and rinsed

I x 400g (I4oz) can of green lentils, drained and rinsed

I onion, roughly chopped

I celery stick, thinly sliced

I red (bell) pepper, roughly chopped

3 tbsp frozen or canned sweetcorn

I rounded tsp mild chilli powder

I tsp smoked paprika

½ tsp dried oregano

pinch of ground cinnamon

pinch of soft light brown sugar

I tbsp barbecue sauce (ensure vegan)

generous pinch of smoked sea salt

handful of flat-leaf parsley, roughly chopped

I   Preheat the oven to 200°C/400°F/gas mark 6.

2   Arrange the sweet potato slices on one or two baking trays, ensuring they don't overlap. Drizzle over the sunflower oil and massage in. Roast in the oven for 20–22 minutes until the edges have browned.

3   Add the chopped tomatoes, kidney beans and green lentils to a large pan, then add the onion, celery, pepper and sweetcorn. Stir in the chilli powder, smoked paprika, oregano, cinnamon and sugar, then bring to the boil over a high heat. Reduce the heat to medium and simmer for 25 minutes.

4   Remove the pan from the heat and stir through the barbecue sauce, sea salt and parsley. Spoon the chilli into bowls or dishes.

5   Remove the sweet potato slices from the oven and place over the chilli. Serve hot.

Speedy Tip

There's no need to add any oil to the chilli pan – it will cook within the tomato base sauce with some simple stirring from you. A drizzle of sunflower oil over the sweet potato topping helps them to crisp up in the oven, in less than 30 minutes.

ROASTED RHUBARB AND STRAWBERRY COMPOTE

SERVES 4

This summery compote is roasted in the oven, to concentrate the seasonal flavours of rhubarb and strawberries. I love how this method keeps the texture of the rhubarb, for a chunky, fresh compote. Serve with cool vegan vanilla yogurt, custard or ice cream, or load over a plant-based pancake.

400g (14oz) rhubarb, chopped into 2cm (¾in) chunks

300g (10oz) strawberries, sliced in half

juice from 1 unwaxed orange

2 tsp caster (superfine) sugar

1 Preheat the oven to 200°C/400°F/gas mark 6.

2 Arrange the rhubarb and strawberries in a deep baking tray and squeeze over the orange juice. Scatter over the sugar.

3 Roast in the oven for 15 minutes, then carefully stir to distribute the juices, and roast for a further 10 minutes. Serve hot or cold.

Speedy Tip

The compote will keep for up to 4 days in the fridge in a sealed jar, and is versatile enough to use for desserts, snacks and breakfast.

SCHOOL-DAYS JAM AND COCONUT SPONGE PUDDING

SERVES 6 ·
SUITABLE FOR FREEZING (CAKE BEFORE TOPPING WITH JAM AND COCONUT)

Transport yourself back to childhood with this classic British school-days pudding. Gently flavoured sponge cake is topped with fruity, slightly tart jam, and topped with sweet coconut. Serve warm with lashings of vegan custard.

250g (2 cups) self-raising flour

100g (½ cup) caster (superfine) sugar

¾ tsp baking powder

250ml (1 cup) sweetened soya milk

100ml (scant ½ cup) sunflower oil

1 tsp vanilla extract

juice of ½ unwaxed lemon

1 rounded tbsp raspberry jam

1 rounded tbsp desiccated (dried shredded) coconut

1   Preheat the oven to 180°C/350°F/gas mark 4. Line a small baking tray (30x20cm/12x8in) with baking parchment.

2   In a large bowl, stir together the flour, sugar and baking powder. In a jug, whisk together the soya milk, sunflower oil, vanilla extract and lemon juice. Fold the liquid mixture into the dry mixture until just combined.

3   Pour into the lined baking tray, then bake in the oven for 20–25 minutes until lightly golden and risen.

4   Remove from the oven and allow to cool for a couple of minutes. Smooth over the jam while the cake is still warm, and sprinkle over the coconut. Best served warm.

Speedy Tip

Feel free to use strawberry or cherry jam, but for nostalgia, opt for raspberry.

RASPBERRY CURD

MAKES 1 SMALL JAR

This sweet and buttery curd has a seasonal twist of fresh raspberries, giving it a fruity flavour and deep pink hue. Use a balloon whisk to get the mixture nice and smooth – and remember that it will thicken as it cools. Delicious drizzled over vegan ice cream, or smoothed onto vegan shortbread.

200g (1¾ cups) raspberries

150g (¾ cup) granulated sugar

400ml (generous 1½ cups) sweetened soya milk

1 tbsp cornflour (cornstarch)

1 tbsp vegan butter

1 Add the raspberries, sugar, soya milk and cornflour to a pan, then bring to a simmer for 15 minutes over a medium heat, whisking frequently to break up the raspberries.

2 Stir in the butter and cook for a further 5 minutes until smooth.

3 Remove from the heat and allow to cool for a few minutes. Place a fine strainer over a large bowl or jug and pour through, pushing with a spatula if needed. Discard the seeds.

4 When the curd is cool, spoon into a clean jar.

Speedy Tip

This raspberry curd will last up to a week in a clean, sealed jar in the fridge.

STICKY GINGER CAKE

SERVES 8 · SUITABLE FOR FREEZING

This dark, sticky cake is infused with spices, rum and black treacle, for a tea time treat that is fiery and delicious. Traditionally, it is cooked in a loaf tin, but as this recipe is quite rich, I recommend that it's cooked in a baking tin and sliced into squares – it will cook more quickly, too.

150g (1¼ cups) plain (all-purpose) flour

1 tsp baking powder

½ tsp bicarbonate of soda (baking soda)

3 tsp ground ginger

1 tsp grated nutmeg

1 tsp ground mixed spice

1 tsp ground cinnamon

50ml (scant ¼ cup) sweetened soya milk

120ml (½ cup) sunflower oil

2 rounded tbsp black treacle

2 rounded tbsp golden syrup, plus extra to serve

2 tbsp vanilla soya yogurt, plus extra to serve

2 tbsp spiced rum (ensure vegan)

1 Preheat the oven to 180°C/350°F/gas mark 4 and line a baking tray (30x20cm/12x8in) with baking parchment.

2 Mix the flour, baking powder, bicarbonate of soda, ginger, nutmeg, mixed spice and cinnamon in a bowl.

3 In a separate large bowl, whisk together the soya milk, sunflower oil, treacle, syrup, soya yogurt and rum until combined. Tip the dry ingredients into the wet mixture and stir together until just combined.

4 Pour into the lined baking tray and bake in the oven for 25–28 minutes. Allow to cool before slicing into 8 squares. Eat plain or serve with a dollop of soya yogurt and an extra drizzle of golden syrup.

Speedy Tip

This cake will last in a sealed container for up to 3 days, but is best eaten fresh.

TRADITIONAL PEANUT BRITTLE

SERVES 4

This sweet treat makes a special homemade gift – if you can bear to share it!
I use salted peanuts in this recipe, to give a moreish salted caramel flavour and
addictive crunch. This peanut brittle will last for up to a week when stored in a
sealed container in a cool place.

250g (1¼ cups) caster
(superfine) sugar

200g (1¼ cups) salted
roasted peanuts

1 Line a large baking tray with baking parchment.

2 Tip the sugar and 100ml (scant ½ cup) of water into
a large pan and bring to the boil over a low heat.
When the sugar has dissolved and the syrup is
simmering, cook for about 10 minutes, stirring the
pan only occasionally until it turns a light caramel
colour.

3 Remove from the heat and stir in the peanuts, then
immediately pour out onto the prepared baking
tray.

4 Allow to set for 15–20 minutes before breaking into
chunks.

Speedy Tip

After 10 minutes of cooking, the hot syrup will be
a gentle caramel colour. Don't allow it to get any
darker or it will taste bitter.

TIMEFRAME INDEX

10-minutes 20–81

blood orange, red cabbage and lentil salad 44

breakfast banana split 24

butternut squash, sage and caramelized onion toastie 43

caponata gnocchi 64

cheat's cherry and chocolate granola crumble 73

chickpea carrot and olive salad 35

Chinese-style hot and sour broth with tofu 46

chocolate hazelnut pots 76

coconut chana masala 70

courgette and red pepper pizza baguettes 63

cream cheese, poppy seed and cucumber toast 31

creamy pea soup with mint and lemon 40

creamy Tuscan beans 58

crispy air fryer salt and pepper tofu 55

egg-less and watercress sandwiches 49

everything tomato sauce 62

frozen yogurt bark 32

garlic broccoli with cashews 52

grilled pineapple sundaes with rum and macadamia nuts 74

lemon, dill and butterbean dip 36

marmalade microwave porridge 28

Mexican-style street corn 38

one-minute cranberry and pecan muesli 27

paprika chickpeas with parsley and lemon 61

pineapple & ginger smoothie 22

sizzling pepper, red onion and black bean fajitas 68

special fried rice 54

spicy peanut stir fry with noodles 67

strawberry and basil cheesecake parfait 80

tagliatelle with cavolo nero, chilli, garlic and lemon 50

two-minute mug carrot cake 79

20-minutes 82–143

aubergine, mushroom and yogurt stroganoff 127

baked bean breakfast quesadillas 92

braised chickpeas with chilli, orange and tomato 113

breakfast bliss bites 87

bruschetta 103

buttered root mash with nutmeg 128

caramelized onion and thyme pinwheels 98

chai-spiced scones 143

chickpea scramble 90

chocolate and banana tortilla pockets 140

courgette pesto 120

creamy mushroom soup 107

easiest-ever Mediterranean bake 130

easy granola 84

falafel tagine 123

grilled aubergine salad 108

grilled peach melba with raspberry sauce 139

hash brown sharer 91

herby spring soup with fregola 110

mango and coconut curry 133

muffin-tin pizza pies 99

PB&J tofu 117

pineapple and black bean tostadas 96

pistachio herb salad 100

pizza pasta 129

rice pudding with cherries 134

roasted tomatoes on toast with salsa verde 88

savoury, smoky yogurt bowls 104

spiced bhaji naan wraps 118

spring orzotto 124

strawberry and cream cheese puffs 136

tamarind, mushroom vand broccoli skewers 114

Tuscan beans with sage 95

30-minutes 144–209

all in one spaghetti bolognese 194

allotment tart 181

apricot, lemon and herb pilaf 166

aubergine and lentil curry 175

aubergine shakshuka with chilli yogurt 148

autumn traybake 185

banana, maple and blueberry baked oats 151

black bean breakfast burritos 153

black pepper crackers 165

breakfast berry Charlotte 146

cheese, spinach and chive muffin frittatas 152

creamy peanut noodle soup 168

crispy popadom Balti pie 191

crispy sweet potato topped chilli 198

frying pan pizza 195

golden quinoa salad 172

harissa chickpea and cauliflower one-pot 186

hearty cobbler with chive dumplings 178

lentil, potato and rosemary soup 154

maple-roasted sweet potato tacos 188

marmalade sausage sandwiches with roasted onions and blackberry pickle 157

nourishing rice bowl 192

raspberry curd 205

rice pop tofu with katsu sauce 197

roasted rhubarb and strawberry compote 200

school-days jam and coconut sponge pudding 202

smoky chipotle mac and cheese 176

spicy pepper, red bean and orange rice pot 182

spicy potato and pea wraps 171

sticky ginger cake 206

sweet chilli cauliflower with crunchy slaw 161

tomato, bean and pasta soup 158

traditional peanut brittle 208

warm asparagus, potato and tomato salad 162

GENERAL INDEX

A

all in one spaghetti bolognese 194

allotment tart 181

almond milk: marmalade microwave porridge 28

almonds
apricot, lemon and herb pilaf 166
easiest-ever Mediterranean bake 130
golden quinoa salad 172

apples: sweet chilli cauliflower with crunchy slaw 161

apricots
apricot, lemon and herb pilaf 166
chickpea carrot and olive salad 35
falafel tagine 123
golden quinoa salad 172
harissa chickpea and cauliflower one-pot 186

asparagus
spring orzotto 124
warm asparagus, potato and tomato salad 162

aubergines (eggplants)
aubergine and lentil curry 175
aubergine, mushroom and yogurt stroganoff 127
aubergine shakshuka with chilli yogurt 148
caponata gnocchi 64
falafel tagine 123
grilled aubergine salad 108

autumn traybake 185

avocados
black bean breakfast burritos 153
golden quinoa salad 172
lunchtime loaded nachos 39
maple-roasted sweet potato tacos 188
nourishing rice bowl 192
pineapple and black bean tostadas 96

sizzling pepper, red onion and black bean fajitas 68

B

baby corns: spicy peanut stir fry with noodles 67

baguettes
bruschetta 103
courgette and red pepper pizza baguettes 63

bake, easiest-ever Mediterranean 130

baked bean breakfast quesadillas 92

Balti pie, crispy popadom 191

bananas
banana, maple and blueberry baked oats 151
breakfast banana split 24
chocolate and banana tortilla pockets 140
frozen yogurt bark 32
pineapple & ginger smoothie 22

barbecue sauce
baked bean breakfast quesadillas 92
Mexican-style street corn 38

bark, frozen yogurt 32

basil
courgette pesto 120
herby spring soup with fregola 110
roasted tomatoes on toast with salsa verde 88
strawberry and basil cheesecake parfait 80

beans 12
creamy Tuscan beans 58
spicy pepper, red bean and orange rice pot 182
tomato, bean and pasta soup 158
Tuscan beans with sage 95

beansprouts: Chinese-style hot and sour broth with tofu 46

berries: breakfast berry Charlotte 146

bhaji: spiced bhaji naan wraps 118

black beans
black bean breakfast burritos 153
pineapple and black bean tostadas 96
sizzling pepper, red onion and black bean fajitas 68

black pepper crackers 165

blackberries
blackberry pickle 157
breakfast berry Charlotte 146

blenders 11

bliss bites, breakfast 87

blood orange, red cabbage and lentil salad 44

blueberries
banana, maple and blueberry baked oats 151
breakfast berry Charlotte 146

bread
breakfast berry Charlotte 146
bruschetta 103
butternut squash, sage and caramelized onion toastie 43
courgette and red pepper pizza baguettes 63
cream cheese, poppy seed and cucumber toast 31
easiest-ever Mediterranean bake 130
egg-less and watercress sandwiches 49
marmalade sausage sandwiches with roasted onions and blackberry pickle 157
roasted tomatoes on toast with salsa verde 88

breakfast banana split 24

breakfast berry Charlotte 146

breakfast bliss bites 87

brittle, traditional peanut 208

broccoli
garlic broccoli with cashews 52
tamarind, mushroom and broccoli skewers 114

broth: Chinese-style hot and sour broth with tofu 46

bruschetta 103

bulgar wheat: pistachio herb salad 100

burritos, black bean breakfast 153

butterbeans: lemon, dill and butterbean dip 36

buttered root mash with nutmeg 128

butternut squash
buttered root mash with nutmeg 128
butternut squash, sage and caramelized onion toastie 43
smoky chipotle mac and cheese 176

C

cabbage
blood orange, red cabbage and lentil salad 44
braised chickpeas with chilli, orange and tomato 113
sweet chilli cauliflower with crunchy slaw 161

cakes
sticky ginger cake 206
two-minute mug carrot cake 79

cannellini beans
creamy Tuscan beans 58
egg-less and watercress sandwiches 49
tomato, bean and pasta soup 158

Tuscan beans with sage 95
capers: roasted tomatoes on toast with salsa verde 88
caponata gnocchi 64
caramelized onion and thyme pinwheels 98
carrots
  all in one spaghetti bolognese 194
  buttered root mash with nutmeg 128
  chickpea carrot and olive salad 35
  Chinese-style hot and sour broth with tofu 46
  creamy peanut noodle soup 168
  crispy popadom Balti pie 191
  falafel tagine 123
  hearty cobbler with chive dumplings 178
  lentil, potato and rosemary soup 154
  nourishing rice bowl 192
  smoky chipotle mac and cheese 176
  special fried rice 54
  spicy peanut stir fry with noodles 67
  sweet chilli cauliflower with crunchy slaw 161
  two-minute mug carrot cake 79
cashews
  garlic broccoli with cashews 52
  special fried rice 54
cauliflower
  crispy popadom Balti pie 191
  harissa chickpea and cauliflower one-pot 186
  sweet chilli cauliflower with crunchy slaw 161
cavolo nero
  tagliatelle with cavolo nero, chilli, garlic and lemon 50
  tomato, bean and pasta soup 158
chai-spiced scones 143
chana masala, coconut 70

Charlotte, breakfast berry 146
cheat's cherry and chocolate granola crumble 73
cheese
  baked bean breakfast quesadillas 92
  courgette pesto 120
  frying pan pizza 195
  lunchtime loaded nachos 39
  muffin-tin pizza pies 99
  pizza pasta 129
  smoky chipotle mac and cheese 176
cheesecake parfait, strawberry and basil 80
cherries
  cheat's cherry and chocolate granola crumble 73
  rice pudding with cherries 134
chickpeas (garbanzo beans)
  braised chickpeas with chilli, orange and tomato 113
  chickpea carrot and olive salad 35
  chickpea scramble 90
  coconut chana masala 70
  falafel tagine 123
  harissa chickpea and cauliflower one-pot 186
  paprika chickpeas with parsley and lemon 61
chilli jam: PB&J tofu 117
chilli sauce: sweet chilli cauliflower with crunchy slaw 161
chillies
  aubergine shakshuka with chilli yogurt 148
  braised chickpeas with chilli, orange and tomato 113
  crispy sweet potato topped chilli 198
  tagliatelle with cavolo nero, chilli, garlic and lemon 50
Chinese-style hot and sour broth with tofu 46

chipotle paste: smoky chipotle mac and cheese 176
chives
  cheese, spinach and chive muffin frittatas 152
  hearty cobbler with chive dumplings 178
chocolate
  breakfast bliss bites 87
  cheat's cherry and chocolate granola crumble 73
  chocolate and banana tortilla pockets 140
  chocolate hazelnut pots 76
chutney: butternut squash, sage and caramelized onion toastie 43
cobbler: hearty cobbler with chive dumplings 178
coconut
  breakfast banana split 24
  frozen yogurt bark 32
  grilled pineapple sundaes with rum and macadamia nuts 74
  school-days jam and coconut sponge pudding 202
coconut milk 15
  coconut chana masala 70
  creamy peanut noodle soup 168
  mango and coconut curry 133
  rice pop tofu with katsu sauce 197
coconut yogurt
  breakfast banana split 24
  spiced bhaji naan wraps 118
  spicy potato and pea wraps 171
  sweet chilli cauliflower with crunchy slaw 161
compote, roasted rhubarb and strawberry 200
containers 11
corn
  Mexican-style street corn 38
  sweetcorn salsa 57

courgettes (zucchini)
  allotment tart 181
  courgette and red pepper pizza baguettes 63
  courgette pesto 120
  herby spring soup with fregola 110
crackers, black pepper 165
cranberries
  easy granola 84
  frozen yogurt bark 32
  golden quinoa salad 172
  one-minute cranberry and pecan muesli 27
cream cheese
  cheese, spinach and chive muffin frittatas 152
  cream cheese, poppy seed and cucumber toast 31
  smoky chipotle mac and cheese 176
  strawberry and basil cheesecake parfait 80
  strawberry and cream cheese puffs 136
creamy mushroom soup 107
creamy pea soup with mint and lemon 40
creamy peanut noodle soup 168
creamy Tuscan beans 58
crispy air fryer salt and pepper tofu 55
crispy popadom Balti pie 191
crispy sweet potato topped chilli 198
crumble, cheat's cherry and chocolate granola 73
crunchy slaw 161
cucumber
  bruschetta 103
  cream cheese, poppy seed and cucumber toast 31
  nourishing rice bowl 192
curd, raspberry 205
curry
  aubergine and lentil curry 175
  coconut chana masala 70
  mango and coconut curry 133

rice pop tofu with katsu
sauce 197
curry pastes 12

D
digestive biscuits (graham
crackers): strawberry
and basil cheesecake
parfait 80
dill
apricot, lemon and herb
pilaf 166
lemon, dill and
butterbean dip 36
dip, lemon, dill and
butterbean 36
drinks: pineapple & ginger
smoothie 22
dumplings, hearty cobbler
with chive 178

E
edamame beans
nourishing rice bowl 192
special fried rice 54
egg-less and watercress
sandwiches 49
everything tomato sauce
62

F
fajitas, sizzling pepper, red
onion and black bean 68
falafel tagine 123
figs: autumn traybake 185
focaccia: easiest-ever
Mediterranean bake 130
freezing food 11
fregola, herby spring soup
with 110
frittatas, cheese, spinach
and chive muffin 152
frozen yogurt bark 32
fruits 16
*see also individual types
of fruit*
frying pan pizza 195

G
garlic
garlic broccoli with
cashews 52
tagliatelle with cavolo
nero, chilli, garlic and
lemon 50

ginger
pineapple & ginger
smoothie 22
sticky ginger cake 206
gnocchi, caponata 64
golden pancakes with
sweetcorn salsa 57
golden quinoa salad 172
granola
cheat's cherry and
chocolate granola
crumble 73
easy granola 84
green beans
creamy Tuscan beans 58
easiest-ever
Mediterranean bake 130
falafel tagine 123
harissa chickpea and
cauliflower one-pot 186
herby spring soup with
fregola 110
mango and coconut
curry 133
spring orzotto 124

H
haricot beans: herby
spring soup with fregola
110
harissa chickpea and
cauliflower one-pot 186
hash brown sharer 91
hazelnuts
breakfast banana split 24
chocolate hazelnut
pots 76
hearty cobbler with chive
dumplings 178
herbs
apricot, lemon and herb
pilaf 166
herby spring soup with
fregola 110
pistachio herb salad 100

I
ice cream
grilled peach melba with
raspberry sauce 139
grilled pineapple
sundaes with rum and
macadamia nuts 74
ingredients 11, 12–16

J
jam: school-days jam and
coconut sponge pudding
202

K
kale: hearty cobbler with
chive dumplings 178
katsu sauce, rice pop tofu
with 197
kitchen hacks 11
kiwi: frozen yogurt bark 32
knives 11

L
leeks
hearty cobbler with
chive dumplings 178
herby spring soup with
fregola 110
lemons
apricot, lemon and herb
pilaf 166
creamy pea soup with
mint and lemon 40
lemon, dill and
butterbean dip 36
paprika chickpeas with
parsley and lemon 61
tagliatelle with cavolo
nero, chilli, garlic and
lemon 50
lentils
all in one spaghetti
bolognese 194
aubergine and lentil
curry 175
blood orange, red
cabbage and lentil
salad 44
crispy sweet potato
topped chilli 198
hearty cobbler with
chive dumplings 178
lentil, potato and
rosemary soup 154
lettuce
golden quinoa salad 172
maple-roasted sweet
potato tacos 188
spiced bhaji naan wraps
118
lunchtime loaded nachos
39

M
mac and cheese, smoky
chipotle 176
macadamia nuts, grilled
pineapple sundaes with
rum and 74
mango and coconut curry
133
mango chutney
coconut chana masala 70
mango and coconut
curry 133
spiced bhaji naan wraps
118
maple syrup
banana, maple and
blueberry baked oats 151
chocolate hazelnut
pots 76
easy granola 84
frozen yogurt bark 32
maple-roasted sweet
potato tacos 188
marmalade
marmalade microwave
porridge 28
marmalade sausage
sandwiches with
roasted onions and
blackberry pickle 157
mayonnaise: egg-less and
watercress sandwiches
49
Mediterranean bake,
easiest-ever 130
Mexican-style street
corn 38
mint
creamy pea soup with
mint and lemon 40
pistachio herb salad 100
muesli, one-minute
cranberry and pecan 27
muffin frittatas, cheese,
spinach and chive 152
muffin-tin pizza pies 99
mug carrot cake, two-
minute 79
mushrooms
aubergine, mushroom
and yogurt stroganoff
127
autumn traybake 185
chickpea scramble 90

Chinese-style hot and
sour broth with tofu 46
courgette and red pepper
pizza baguettes 63
creamy mushroom soup
107
muffin-tin pizza pies 99
pizza pasta 129
tamarind, mushroom
and broccoli skewers 114

N
naan bread
spiced bhaji naan wraps
118
spicy potato and pea
wraps 171
nachos, lunchtime loaded
39
non-dairy ingredients 16
noodles 12
creamy peanut noodle
soup 168
spicy peanut stir fry with
noodles 67
nourishing rice bowl 192
nutmeg, buttered root
mash with 128

O
oats
banana, maple and
blueberry baked oats 151
breakfast banana split 24
breakfast bliss bites 87
easy granola 84
one-minute cranberry
and pecan muesli 27
oils 15
olives
bruschetta 103
caponata gnocchi 64
chickpea carrot and olive
salad 35
easiest-ever
Mediterranean bake 130
lunchtime loaded
nachos 39
paprika chickpeas with
parsley and lemon 61
pizza pasta 129
one-minute cranberry and
pecan muesli 27
one-pot, harissa chickpea
and cauliflower 186

onions
butternut squash, sage
and caramelized onion
toastie 43
caramelized onion and
thyme pinwheels 98
marmalade sausage
sandwiches with
roasted onions and
blackberry pickle 157
sizzling pepper, red
onion and black bean
fajitas 68
spiced bhaji naan wraps
118
oranges
blood orange, red
cabbage and lentil
salad 44
braised chickpeas with
chilli, orange and
tomato 113
spicy pepper, red bean
and orange rice pot 182
orzotto, spring 124
oven temperatures 11

P
pancakes: golden
pancakes with
sweetcorn salsa 57
paprika chickpeas with
parsley and lemon 61
parfait, strawberry and
basil cheesecake 80
parsley
apricot, lemon and herb
pilaf 166
paprika chickpeas with
parsley and lemon 61
pistachio herb salad 100
roasted tomatoes on
toast with salsa verde
88
parsnips: buttered root
mash with nutmeg 128
pasta 12
all in one spaghetti
bolognese 194
herby spring soup with
fregola 110
pizza pasta 129
smoky chipotle mac
and cheese 176
spring orzotto 124

tagliatelle with cavolo
nero, chilli, garlic and
lemon 50
tomato, bean and pasta
soup 158
pastry, shop-bought 16
PB&J tofu 117
peaches: grilled peach
melba with raspberry
sauce 139
peanut butter
breakfast bliss bites 87
creamy peanut noodle
soup 168
PB&J tofu 117
spicy peanut stir fry with
noodles 67
peanuts
spicy peanut stir fry with
noodles 67
traditional peanut brittle
208
peas
creamy pea soup with
mint and lemon 40
crispy popadom Balti
pie 191
special fried rice 54
spicy potato and pea
wraps 171
spring orzotto 124
pecans
banana, maple and
blueberry baked oats 151
easy granola 84
one-minute cranberry
and pecan muesli 27
peppers
all in one spaghetti
bolognese 194
allotment tart 181
aubergine shakshuka
with chilli yogurt 148
black bean breakfast
burritos 153
bruschetta 103
courgette and red
pepper pizza baguettes
63
crispy popadom Balti
pie 191
crispy sweet potato
topped chilli 198
easiest-ever
Mediterranean bake 130

falafel tagine 123
lunchtime loaded
nachos 39
paprika chickpeas with
parsley and lemon 61
pizza pasta 129
savoury, smoky yogurt
bowls 104
sizzling pepper, red
onion and black bean
fajitas 68
smoky chipotle mac and
cheese 176
spicy pepper, red bean
and orange rice pot 182
sweetcorn salsa 57
pesto, courgette 120
pickle, blackberry 157
pies
crispy popadom Balti
pie 191
muffin-tin pizza pies 99
pilaf, apricot, lemon and
herb 166
pine nuts
autumn traybake 185
chickpea carrot and olive
salad 35
courgette pesto 120
savoury, smoky yogurt
bowls 104
pineapple
grilled pineapple
sundaes with rum and
macadamia nuts 74
pineapple and black
bean tostadas 96
pineapple & ginger
smoothie 22
pinwheels, caramelized
onion and thyme 98
pistachios
blood orange, red
cabbage and lentil
salad 44
pistachio herb salad 100
pizza
courgette and red
pepper pizza baguettes
63
frying pan pizza 195
muffin-tin pizza pies 99
pizza pasta 129
pomegranate

blood orange, red cabbage and lentil salad 44
grilled aubergine salad 108
popadoms: crispy popadom Balti pie 191
poppy seeds: cream cheese, poppy seed and cucumber toast 31
porridge, marmalade microwave 28
potatoes
  crispy popadom Balti pie 191
  hash brown sharer 91
  lentil, potato and rosemary soup 154
  smoky chipotle mac and cheese 176
  spicy potato and pea wraps 171
  warm asparagus, potato and tomato salad 162
puff pastry
  allotment tart 181
  caramelized onion and thyme pinwheels 98
  strawberry and cream cheese puffs 136
pulses 12
pumpkin seeds
  easy granola 84
  nourishing rice bowl 192
  one-minute cranberry and pecan muesli 27

Q
quesadillas, baked bean breakfast 92
quinoa: golden quinoa salad 172

R
radishes
  nourishing rice bowl 192
  pineapple and black bean tostadas 96
raisin and cinnamon loaf: breakfast berry Charlotte 146
raspberries
  breakfast berry Charlotte 146

grilled peach melba with raspberry sauce 139
raspberry curd 205
red kidney beans
  crispy sweet potato topped chilli 198
  lunchtime loaded nachos 39
  spicy pepper, red bean and orange rice pot 182
rhubarb: roasted rhubarb and strawberry compote 200
rice
  apricot, lemon and herb pilaf 166
  nourishing rice bowl 192
  rice pudding with cherries 134
  special fried rice 54
  spicy pepper, red bean and orange rice pot 182
rice pop tofu with katsu sauce 197
rocket (arugula)
  grilled aubergine salad 108
  warm asparagus, potato and tomato salad 162
rosemary: lentil, potato and rosemary soup 154
rum: grilled pineapple sundaes with rum and macadamia nuts 74

S
sage
  butternut squash, sage and caramelized onion toastie 43
  Tuscan beans with sage 95
salads
  blood orange, red cabbage and lentil salad 44
  chickpea carrot and olive salad 35
  crunchy slaw 161
  golden quinoa salad 172
  grilled aubergine salad 108
  pistachio herb salad 100
  warm asparagus, potato and tomato salad 162

salsa
  black bean breakfast burritos 153
  sweetcorn salsa 57
salsa verde, roasted tomatoes on toast with 88
salt 15
sandwiches
  egg-less and watercress sandwiches 49
  marmalade sausage sandwiches with roasted onions and blackberry pickle 157
sauce, everything tomato 62
sausages: marmalade sausage sandwiches with roasted onions and blackberry pickle 157
savoury, smoky yogurt bowls 104
school-days jam and coconut sponge pudding 202
scones, chai-spiced 143
sesame seeds
  breakfast bliss bites 87
  nourishing rice bowl 192
  sweet chilli cauliflower with crunchy slaw 161
shakshuka: aubergine shakshuka with chilli yogurt 148
sizzling pepper, red onion and black bean fajitas 68
skewers, tamarind, mushroom and broccoli 114
slaw, crunchy 161
smoky chipotle mac and cheese 176
smoothie, pineapple & ginger 22
soups
  Chinese-style hot and sour broth with tofu 46
  creamy mushroom soup 107
  creamy pea soup with mint and lemon 40
  creamy peanut noodle soup 168

herby spring soup with fregola 110
lentil, potato and rosemary soup 154
tomato, bean and pasta soup 158
soya milk
  raspberry curd 205
  rice pudding with cherries 134
soya yogurt
  aubergine, mushroom and yogurt stroganoff 127
  aubergine shakshuka with chilli yogurt 148
  frozen yogurt bark 32
  harissa chickpea and cauliflower one-pot 186
  savoury, smoky yogurt bowls 104
  strawberry and basil cheesecake parfait 80
spaghetti bolognese, all in one 194
special fried rice 54
spice blends 12
spiced bhaji naan wraps 118
spicy peanut stir fry with noodles 67
spicy pepper, red bean and orange rice pot 182
spicy potato and pea wraps 171
spinach
  baked bean breakfast quesadillas 92
  black bean breakfast burritos 153
  cheese, spinach and chive muffin frittatas 152
  chickpea scramble 90
  creamy Tuscan beans 58
  paprika chickpeas with parsley and lemon 61
  pineapple & ginger smoothie 22
sponge pudding, school-days jam and coconut 202
spring orzotto 124
squash

buttered root mash with
nutmeg 128
butternut squash, sage
and caramelized onion
toastie 43
smoky chipotle mac and
cheese 176
sticky ginger cake 206
stir fry: spicy peanut stir
fry with noodles 67
store cupboard essentials
11, 12–16
strawberries
breakfast berry
Charlotte 146
roasted rhubarb and
strawberry compote
200
strawberry and basil
cheesecake parfait 80
strawberry and cream
cheese puffs 136
stroganoff, aubergine,
mushroom and yogurt
127
sugarsnap peas
creamy peanut noodle
soup 168
special fried rice 54
spicy peanut stir fry with
noodles 67
sultanas (golden raisins)
chai-spiced scones 143
marmalade microwave
porridge 28
two-minute mug carrot
cake 79
sundaes: grilled pineapple
sundaes with rum and
macadamia nuts 74
swede (rutabaga):
buttered root mash with
nutmeg 128
sweet chilli cauliflower
with crunchy slaw 161
sweet potatoes
autumn traybake 185
black bean breakfast
burritos 153
crispy sweet potato
topped chilli 198
maple-roasted sweet
potato tacos 188
savoury, smoky yogurt
bowls 104

sweetcorn
crispy sweet potato
topped chilli 198
Mexican-style street
corn 38
muffin-tin pizza pies 99
sweetcorn salsa 57

T
tacos, maple-roasted
sweet potato 188
tagine, falafel 123
tagliatelle with cavolo
nero, chilli, garlic and
lemon 50
tahini: golden quinoa
salad 172
tamarind, mushroom and
broccoli skewers 114
tart, allotment 181
Tenderstem broccoli:
tamarind, mushroom
and broccoli skewers 114
thyme: caramelized onion
and thyme pinwheels 98
toast
bruschetta 103
cream cheese, poppy
seed and cucumber
toast 31
roasted tomatoes on
toast with salsa verde
88
toastie, butternut squash,
sage and caramelized
onion 43
tofu 16
cheese, spinach and
chive muffin frittatas
152
Chinese-style hot and
sour broth with tofu 46
chocolate hazelnut
pots 76
crispy air fryer salt and
pepper tofu 55
egg-less and watercress
sandwiches 49
PB&J tofu 117
rice pop tofu with katsu
sauce 197
tomatoes 12
all in one spaghetti
bolognese 194
allotment tart 181

aubergine shakshuka
with chilli yogurt 148
braised chickpeas with
chilli, orange and
tomato 113
bruschetta 103
caponata gnocchi 64
chickpea scramble 90
courgette and red
pepper pizza baguettes
63
creamy Tuscan beans 58
crispy popadom Balti
pie 191
crispy sweet potato
topped chilli 198
easiest-ever
Mediterranean bake 130
everything tomato sauce
62
falafel tagine 123
frying pan pizza 195
grilled aubergine salad
108
harissa chickpea and
cauliflower one-pot 186
hearty cobbler with
chive dumplings 178
lunchtime loaded
nachos 39
muffin-tin pizza pies 99
paprika chickpeas with
parsley and lemon 61
pistachio herb salad 100
pizza pasta 129
roasted tomatoes on
toast with salsa verde
88
spicy pepper, red bean
and orange rice pot 182
sweetcorn salsa 57
tomato, bean and pasta
soup 158
Tuscan beans with sage
95
warm asparagus, potato
and tomato salad 162
tortilla wraps
baked bean breakfast
quesadillas 92
black bean breakfast
burritos 153
chocolate and banana
tortilla pockets 140
lunchtime loaded
nachos 39

muffin-tin pizza pies 99
pineapple and black
bean tostadas 96
sizzling pepper, red
onion and black bean
fajitas 68
tostadas, pineapple and
black bean 96
traybake, autumn 185
Tuscan beans
creamy Tuscan beans 58
Tuscan beans with sage
95
two-minute mug carrot
cake 79

V
vegetables 15
see also individual types
of vegetable

W
water chestnuts: Chinese-
style hot and sour broth
with tofu 46
watercress: egg-less and
watercress sandwiches
49
wraps
spiced bhaji naan wraps
118
spicy potato and pea
wraps 171

Y
yogurt
aubergine, mushroom
and yogurt stroganoff
127
aubergine shakshuka
with chilli yogurt 148
breakfast banana split 24
frozen yogurt bark 32
harissa chickpea and
cauliflower one-pot 186
savoury, smoky yogurt
bowls 104
spiced bhaji naan wraps
118
spicy potato and pea
wraps 171
strawberry and basil
cheesecake parfait 80
sweet chilli cauliflower
with crunchy slaw 161

AUTHOR BIOGRAPHY

Katy Beskow is an award-winning cook, writer and cookery tutor with a passion for seasonal ingredients, vibrant food and fuss-free home cooking. Once inspired by a bustling and colourful fruit market in South London, Katy now lives in rural Yorkshire and cooks from a small (yet perfectly functioning) kitchen.

She blogs at www.katybeskow.com. Katy is the author of *15-Minute Vegan* (2017), *15-Minute Vegan Comfort Food* (2018), *15-Minute Vegan on a Budget* (2019), *Five Ingredient Vegan* (2019), *Vegan Fakeaway* (2020), *Easy Vegan Bible* (2020), *Vegan Roasting Pan* (2021) and *Vegan BBQ* (2022); this is her ninth book.

ACKNOWLEDGEMENTS

What a pleasure it has been to write *Easy Speedy Vegan*, creating recipes to suit you, and your lifestyle.

Huge thank you to the editorial team at Quadrille Publishing. Thank you to publishing director Sarah Lavelle for all of the incredible opportunities over the past 6 years. Special thanks to commissioning editor Harriet Webster for believing in this project, attention to detail, and support throughout. Thank you to copy editor Clare Sayer for the editorial support. It is a privilege, as always, to work with you all.

Thank you to designer Emily Lapworth and team for the art direction and design. This truly is a beautiful book.

Massive thanks to photographer Luke Albert, food stylist Tamara Vos, assistant food stylist Charlotte Whatcott, and prop stylist Louie Waller, for the shoots in both South London and Kent. It was great to be able to join you in person again – always a highlight of the project!

Thank you to publicity manager Rebecca Smedley for your ongoing hard work with all of the book campaigns. A big thanks to marketing executive Laura Eldridge for your expertise throughout the process.

Huge thanks, as always, to my fabulous literary agent, Victoria Hobbs and the team at A.M. Health. I am so grateful for your knowledge, support and guidance. Thank you for believing in me, then and now.

Thank you to my wonderful friends Mary-Anne, Emma, Charlotte, Louise, Amelia, Amy, Katie and Neil. Looking forward to a catch up with you all soon.

To my lovely and ever-supportive family: Mum, Dad, Carolyne and Mark. Thank you for your encouragement and kindness, I hope you enjoy this book. Thank you to my beautiful twin nieces Tamzin and Tara who fill me with inspiration, happiness and joy. Thank you to Auntie May for your kind words and support throughout the process. Thank you to Pandi, the house rabbit, for your companionship and cuddles.